LOVE IN 'BOMB CITY'

Also by Ben Forde

Hope in 'Bomb City' (with Chris Spencer)

Love in 'Bomb City'

Ben Forde
with Chris Spencer

Marshalls

Marshalls Paperbacks
Marshall, Morgan & Scott

1 Bath Street, London EC1V 9LB

Reprinted
Impression no. 10 9 8 7 6 5 4 3 2 - 86 85 84 83 82

The names of some of the characters in this book have
been changed.

ISBN 0 551 00956 X

Printed in Great Britain by Hazell Watson and Viney,
Aylesbury.

Contents

DEDICATED TO
Aunt Sarah
and
David and Gillian

1: The lights of home

One thing about living in Northern Ireland: when your work takes you on a long journey across the province you can be sure that you'll be passing through some beautiful scenery. Whichever direction you take you can count on picture postcard views: the quiet calm of the loughs . . . the sturdy magnificence of the mountains . . . the lush greenery of the valleys . . . the gentle ruggedness of the coastline . . . Always there's something to see. Sometimes it's the full-blown panoramic canvas, like the sweeping vision of a valley seen from the mountain road, and sometimes the isolated little cameo, like the sun-dappled vista of a bubbling stream framed within the solid archway of a stone bridge.

Yes, always something to see, and always a reminder that despite the ugly deeds of the men of violence God's love is constant. As permanent as the hills. And as I drove home to Belfast from the 'bandit country' of Armagh on that hazy summer evening, my mind still reeling from the sickening sight of two young soldiers who'd been blasted to death on a country road by an IRA bomb, it was with gratitude that I was able to dwell upon the verse of Scripture that had come to me as I'd looked away from the grim scene of murder to the distant slopes from where the explosives had been detonated: 'I will lift up mine eyes unto the hills, from whence cometh my help. My help cometh from the Lord, who made heaven and earth.'

More hills were in sight as I turned the last corner, but now my mind was upon another great source of inspiration and peace. Directly ahead of me a gentle brightness shone through the summer dusk: the lights of home. To me that is a precious sight.

Beside the gate, Shane, our red setter, stirred to the familiar sound of the car, and from the side of the house our daughter Keri came trundling out on roller-skates, smiling and waving.

Yes, it was good to be home, and good to know that I had the next few days off. The house needed a lick of paint here and there, and the garden needed attention, too; little jobs which I would enjoy because they were so far removed from the police work that normally filled my days, and because home is where I love to be. In a land like ours, where there is so much unrest, so much violence, a member of the security forces needs a mental oasis to which he or she can return for rest and refreshment from the heat of the day's troubles, and for me that oasis is found in home life.

Indoors, Lily was preparing the tea and young Clive was curled up in his favourite armchair in front of the TV set waiting for the news programme to end and a cartoon feature to begin. I stood in the doorway, watching with a whole jumble of feelings as the news cameras suddenly transported me back to the awful scene that had crowded my senses just a few short hours earlier: the twisted wreckage of the army patrol van, the enormous crater left by the bomb-blast, the debris and the uprooted trees, the police officers sealing off the road. . .

Suddenly Lily was at my side, drying her hands on a kitchen towel and shaking her head at the callous murders. The two soldiers who died were aged nineteen; their lives had barely begun.

'Did they say Armagh?' Lily asked.

I nodded, but did not look at her. 'I was there,' I said. But it wasn't until much later that I told her I'd twice driven over the culvert where the bomb was concealed, the second time less than twenty minutes before the explosion. Fortunately, my colleagues and I had been travelling in an unmarked car. Otherwise, who knows? – perhaps the terrorists would have picked on us. They were in hiding away across the field, watching and waiting for a likely target for their remote-controlled bomb.

But life has to go on. I turned to Lily. 'Do I have time to walk the dog, love, or is tea nearly ready?'

'No, you go on ahead, Ben; I'll be another twenty minutes yet.' She turned to Clive. 'Do you want to go with Daddy, Clive, or are you watching your programme?'

Clive decided to give his cartoon a miss and we headed out for the fields together . . . the two of us and Shane.

Did I say I would walk the dog? With Shane it's more a case of the dog walking me. When he's eager for a run it's a relief when we reach the fields and I can let him off the leash, for he's a big and powerful animal and will have you off your feet if he decides to charge away when you're not taking the strain on the lead. Mind you, when we're out jogging and have a hill to cope with, Shane's strength can be a distinct advantage. The one holding on to his lead is always the first to the top!

But on this evening there were no hills; just the flowing fields, the evening sun, the still air . . . and time to think.

Away down the path Clive was teasing Shane and then they were rolling on the grassy floor, wrestling – boy and dog locked in playful combat, arms and legs flailing, laughter mingling with excited barking, the sounds of fun carrying across the open land. I stood back, watching with a smile, grateful for the sheer innocence of the moment; thankful for the sanity of it. For this was a little oasis in itself – a wee pool of peace after the rigours of a day of violence.

Standing there on the gentle earth, the evening sun

still warm on my back, I was conscious of the enormous contrast between this scene and that which had filled my eyes hours earlier down in Armagh. So strong was the contrast, in fact, that it seemed almost impossible that the two should be able to exist side by side . . . and for a fleeting moment on that golden evening it seemed as though one of them must be unreal, existing only in a dream. Or a nightmare.

But no, the terror was real enough. For twenty-two years I'd been a serving member of the RUC (Royal Ulster Constabulary) and for a total of eighteen of those years my country had endured various terrorist campaigns. In my entire career as a police officer I had known only four years of normality.

Oh yes, the terror was real all right. Since the present troubles had begun in Northern Ireland more than two thousand people had died in gun and bomb attacks, more than six hundred of those being my colleagues in the security forces. Countless others had been injured. And as for the civilian population – well, I doubt if there remained a family in the province that had not been affected, either directly or indirectly. And how we had wept! Between us we must have shed enough tears to fill the Irish Sea. Our gravediggers probably had shifted enough earth to build a mountain. And surely a whole forest of timber had gone into all the coffins needed to lay our loved ones to rest.

And now, today, on a country road awash in the August sunlight, the IRA had pressed a button and pushed up the death toll by two. Oh, they would have preferred more, but not bad for an afternoon's work.

What *was* this madness that had gripped our land? And what was I doing in the middle of it, chasing after the perpetrators of these crimes, spending hour after hour in the interrogation room with men who, given half the chance, would cut my throat? It was crazy, absolutely crazy. This wasn't what I had joined the police for . . .

And while a boy and a dog rolled happily on the grass in the late sun, I was travelling back through the years to a very different scene . . . to a cold, clear February morning when our street was bathed in pale sunlight and the frost sparkled on the pavements and crackled under our shoes . . .

I stood at the gate and watched with the silent houses as Dad steered his old bike around the ice patches and blew little clouds of steam into the sharp air. Before he reached the corner he turned his head and called out in soft, scarf-muffled tones: 'Bye, son. See you.'

Indoors, my sister Leah was just getting up. Through the ceiling I could hear her humming to herself as she got ready for work, and soon she appeared, still humming, at the foot of the stairs. She was surprised to see me up and dressed.

'I thought you'd be having a lie in,' she said. 'Your bus doesn't leave till half ten, does it?'

'Couldn't sleep,' I said. 'You know how it is, new job and all.'

'And what a job, eh? Our Ben a policeman! My, those criminals had better watch out now, eh, Mum?'

Mum, sitting in the chair to which rheumatoid arthritis confined her, smiled but said nothing. Inside she was wrestling with apprehension. And who could blame her? Here was her only son leaving home to start what amounted to a new life. But more than that, it was a life that would know danger – even the risk of death. It was no use trying to play these things down, as though they hardly ever happened. The radio and newspapers told a different story. There was an IRA campaign going on. Policemen were being killed.

But even on that last morning, Mum never said a word to discourage me. She knew that at nineteen I was responsible enough to be making my own decisions, and she would not seek to preserve the life she had nurtured from the womb by holding it to herself any longer. She was a good and wise mother; she knew that I had my own life to lead. Besides, long ago – many years before I had told her of my ambition to join the RUC – she had committed my life to God, and she knew that I too now loved the Lord. If this was the way he was leading me, how could she interfere? There is no safer or better place than the palm of God's hand.

On the way to the bus station in Portadown's Market Street an old fellow – one of the locals – nodded towards my suitcase. 'And where be you off to, young Ben?' he enquired.

'The Police Training College at Enniskillen,' Mr. Skinner.

'Then hurry up and get trained and catch them terrorists.'

'I'll do my best, sir.'

The same conversation must have taken place at least half a dozen times that morning, but I didn't mind; I was glad to feel the support of the townspeople. It gave an identity to 'the public' whom this young man was to be trained to protect. Ordinary, good-living people who wished harm on no one but whose peace and safety were being threatened by a troublesome section of our community who refused to let the past die and would stop at nothing to rid the country of the British and restore a united Ireland. I realised that by enrolling as a policeman I was identifying myself with the British government which the terrorists so loathed, and by this act I was making myself their enemy. That was a strange thought and an uncomfortable one; it brought with it a sense of isolation, and somehow it seemed terribly unfair. I was joining the police force to be a servant of the people, not a soldier at arms. Oh well, maybe this terrorist campaign wouldn't go on much longer. Who was to say that by the time my six months' training was over things wouldn't have quietened down? One could live in hopes . . .

The tortured yelp of an indignant red setter burst into my reverie (Clive had trodden on his tail!) and Shane came bounding towards me, then hurtled past, obviously having decided it was time his master was getting back.

'Come on, Clive,' I called. 'Let's get some tea.'

He jumped to his feet and fell into a run, galloping after Shane, leaving me to follow on behind with nothing but the shadows of a distant world for company . . .

Yes, we could live in hopes, but apart from a brief respite in the mid-sixties when the IRA was inactive, those hopes remained unfulfilled. The terror went on, year in, year out, and the casualties mounted. No, this wasn't what I had joined the police for – but, for the present at least, it was what I was stuck with. Making sense of it, though, was something else. How could I make sense of a hole fourteen feet deep where, only minutes before, a culvert had been? Or a mangled army vehicle with the bodies of two young men inside? Or a telephone call to the newspapers proudly claiming 'Our group was responsible'? And how could I make sense of the fact that a CID officer by the name of Ben Forde was on the scene, doing what little he could to assist?

Too often I have driven home with the ugly memories of such slaughter in my mind, and too often I have found myself asking, 'Why, Lord?' Not only, Why did it happen? But, Why did you want me there? And I must admit that it is not very often that the answer is revealed. But I do know that in the divine scheme of things there is a reason for everything that touches the life of God's children, and that when we are obedient to him and following his pre-ordained plan for our lives, blessing will flow. More often than not we shall be unaware of it, but nevertheless it will be there. Sometimes, however, our Lord allows us a glimpse behind the scenes, and then perhaps we begin to see how he is working out his purposes . . . and why he has led us a certain way.

Fourteen months after the death of these young soldiers, and ten months after the publication of my first book, *Hope in 'Bomb City'*, I received a letter which shone a little light into the darkness of that situation. It came from a lady in Scotland who had read the book, and in her letter she wrote:

'The job you do in the RUC must at times be so heart-breaking, especially after reading about the murders of your friend Neville and Inspector Bell. I could feel the grief and hurt you were describing because my family and I have had our own share of it. You see, my brother, Gunner Richard Furminger, was killed in Northern Ireland whilst on active service, on August 2 last year. He was aged almost twenty. I was wondering if the murder of the soldiers you refer to in the postscript of your book was that of my brother and young Paul Reeve? If it was, then it is a blessing to know that God-fearing, capable policemen like yourself were around to aid and comfort the other members of Richard's tragedy who survived.'

I was able to write back, confirming that this lady's brother was indeed one of the two soldiers who died in that explosion. I also thanked her for her letter because, without realising it, she had done more for me than I had been able to do for her. It was a simple thing, but her expression of appreciation that a Christian had been at the scene of her brother's death meant a lot to me. Such involvement with the grisly deeds of the terrorist was not at all what I had in mind when I had set out on my career with the constabulary all those years ago. By choice I would transfer to another, less unpleasant branch of police work tomorrow. Our ways, of course, are not always God's ways . . . but his ways are always the best. And when the going gets tough I find myself returning in my thoughts to that last morning at home in Portadown so many years ago, and to the text which God gave me as the watchword for my new life of service in the RUC: 'Trust in the Lord with all thine heart and lean not unto thine own understanding. In all thy ways acknowledge him, and he shall direct thy paths.'

His wisdom does not tarnish with the years.

2: Voices from the past

In Northern Ireland we live with the past in our pocket. It's something we always carry around with us. For the terrorist, of course, it's the injustices of history that perpetually fuel his campaign of violence, while for those who have lost loved ones or friends by the bullet or the bomb, the past is always alive in our memories of those dear ones no longer with us. Day by day, as we act out the drama of our lives, they are there in the wings – gentle ghosts, ever ready to play their part in familiar scenes, to whisper their lines in oft rehearsed situations, or simply to swell the crowd of extras on a stage now deprived of their presence in a leading role.

For me the drama revolves around my police work, and the missing member of the cast is a man called Neville Cummings. In *Hope in 'Bomb City'* I told how my relationship with Neville developed over the five years that we worked together, sharing the same desk and performing the same duties, and how, on a black Thursday night, my friend died as the result of a booby-trap explosion.

For Neville, who was also a fellow believer in Jesus Christ, it is a case of 'absent from the body, present with the Lord', but for me and my close colleagues there is a sense in which Neville is still with us; such a man is not forgotten. And from time to time the memory of him will spring from the shadows of the mind into the full glare of the spotlight . . .

16

It was a brisk, breezy day in March – the sort of day that hangs on to the tail of winter with one hand and reaches out for spring with the other. I'd reported to police headquarters early in the morning, but for once there was no immediate business. A call would need to be made to my old station at Donegall Pass, however. I turned to John, my immediate superior and a good friend.

'Do you fancy a run downtown?'

'Why not?' he said – and then our colleague Noel piped up:

'Hey, that's a grand idea. I'm just off duty. Maybe you can drop me off at Bradbury Place. I need to get some trousers.'

There was no rush to get to Donegall Pass so we decided to accompany Noel on his sartorial mission . . . but we soon wished we hadn't! Noel has one of those annoyingly trim, athletic figures that remains constant, regardless of cream buns and stodgy puddings, while the rest of us seem to put on pounds at the merest whiff of a doughnut! So when Noel goes shopping for trousers he heads for the youngsters' boutique where he slides effortlessly into all the off-the-peg slimline styles . . . while the more substantial among us hover awkwardly in the corner, simply itching to make our escape from a seemingly undernourished world where the assistants don't bother to approach with a courteous 'Can I help you?' because they need only one look to know they can't!

At last we were able to retreat, vowing never again to look a potato in the eye, while Noel bid us farewell, tucking his miniscule purchase under his arm and smiling the smug smile of the innocent.

Out in the street the sun struggled to warm us while a blustery March wind came bullying round us, driving us on towards Donegall Pass. In a cloud of swirling city dust we blew out of Bradbury Place, glancing to our right into Botanic Avenue, and as my eyes fell upon the distant zebra crossing I was momentarily transported in my thoughts to a similarly bright April day way back in 1974 . . . a warm, dreamlike day that dissolved into nightmare when the sunny peace that had settled on the city was suddenly shattered by the panic cry: 'A bomb! There's a bomb in Botanic Avenue!'

We stepped quickly across the road, the picture memories swirling through my mind: pictures of me running with a uniformed colleague through the sunshine, haring into Botanic Avenue and shouting the warning to the milling crowds; pictures of the white-faced shoppers hurrying to evacuate the area, and the anxious shopkeepers searching their premises for an unclaimed bag or box that might contain the hidden explosives.

As we pressed on I recalled searching the parked vehicles in the street, all to no avail, while additional RUC men were drafted in to seal off the area and redirect the traffic. The search had continued, but still no bomb. Then our suspicions had been aroused by a van parked just round the corner in Posnett Street – a van left with its window open. Cautiously, we'd investigated . . . and discovered the bitter-sweet smell of almond given off by gelignite. In the back we had uncovered two parcels beneath a tarpaulin – and then the terror had struck!

The pictures came more quickly now: we were racing from the scene, shouting our warning, but suddenly we saw traffic heading down Posnett Street and I had turned and run back to warn the drivers of the danger.

Then came the explosion: a horrendous bang and an invisible shock-wave that tossed me into the air and left me lying on the warm pavement, pains pounding my head and back as I gazed up into a circle of faces . . .

I had been only eight feet from the van when that bomb went off, but thankfully I was shielded from the full force of the blast by a passing lorry.

A close call! The closest, in fact, that I'd ever experienced – and one that I'm not likely to forget.

The memories were to continue flowing that afternoon, for Donegall Pass was where Neville and I were based during our five years together and where he met his death. It is also where I was serving when I recorded my first album of gospel songs and when I was active in the RUC choir. I was reminded of this because as John and I went up the station's three flights of stairs I found myself taking advantage of the stair-well's excellent acoustics (better than any concert hall!) with a quick burst of a song. I used to do this a lot when I was stationed here, and I remember Neville laughing his gentle laugh and pulling my leg when we passed on those stairs. I have never had any illusions about my singing voice, but even if I had I think that Neville, being the good friend that he was, would have seen to it that I kept my feet firmly on the ground. And as John and I entered the office where we had business that day – the very office where Neville and I used to share a desk – another of those picture memories came leaping out of my sub-conscious.

Over at the window I glanced down to where my car was parked in the station yard. Neville had helped me choose that car all those years ago and together we had clocked up many thousands of miles in it. One day, shortly after that first album had been released, I had just parked the car (as it happened, in the very space that I'd driven into earlier that morning) and as I switched off the engine I turned to Neville with the question that had been hovering on my lips throughout our journey that day; a question which had managed to dodge being asked so far, perhaps because I was afraid of what the answer might be.

I turned to my old friend. 'Did you, er – did you play the record?'

He looked at me, a grin rising in his eyes. 'I did.'

'Well, what did you think?' I said, grinning myself.

He laughed shortly. 'Well, to be honest – not too hot.'

You could always count on Neville to hit the nail on the head.

I turned from the window – and there was our old desk; the desk at which Neville had been working that night when an officer brought in a shotgun found in a back yard after an anonymous tip-off . . . a booby-trapped shotgun which exploded when it was broken open. Inspector George Bell, who had been holding the gun, died instantly. Neville lost his life after being struck by flying debris. He left a wife, Avril, and three lovely kids.

Lily and I still keep in touch with the family. One night we took a drive out to their modest little home in Newtownbreda to drop off some sheet music which sixteen-year-old Sharon had asked me to obtain for her. We took some chocolates, too, and had little difficulty in persuading young Andrew (he's thirteen now) to hand them round! Peter, nineteen and the image of his Dad, launched into conversation over our mutual love of football while Lily and Avril disappeared into the kitchen to brew up some tea.

And thus we passed a pleasant hour together. Yet even as we talked I was aware of the loss of husband and father which is still felt in this home. How could it be any other way? Neville was a home-loving family man and now the family is incomplete. Yes, the husband and father is still sorely missed, but clearly, with God's help, they are coping, and later on that evening, as Lily and I pulled away in the car, my mind ran back to Avril's words two years earlier: 'God has been so faithful. You know, we've always had enough for our everyday needs, and to spare. And I've become so assured of his love and care for us day by day that, although I still don't understand it, I'm aware that he did know best; he does do all things well . . .

'Ben, it's a hard road to travel, but when you reach this point you find that your heavenly Father undertakes in everything.'

Avril imparted this and other thoughts in *Hope in 'Bomb City'* and her story was to be appreciated by many, not least by a young widow and mother who attended the same church as Avril and who identified with much of what she had shared because her own husband had been a member of the RUC, and he too had died at the hands of the terrorists. His name was Gerald Davidson and the story of how I came to include him in this book is the story of how God put tears in my eyes for a man I had never met . . .

3: Faith under fire

At around two-thirty on the afternoon of Sunday, October 28, 1979, a police Land-Rover reversed out of Springfield Road RUC Station in answer to a call from the nearby Royal Victoria Hospital. As the driver swung the vehicle round, gunfire exploded from a house across the road. Terrorists had taken over a terraced home and had lain in wait for a suitable target to attack. They had chosen well. The Land-Rover was packed with a full complement of six police officers and a soldier. As high-velocity bullets ripped through the vehicle's steel-plating the soldier was killed instantly and three RUC men were badly wounded. One of them, Gerald Davidson, was struck in the neck. It was his first day back on duty after a week's leave.

Three weeks later, almost to the hour, I received a telephone call at home from the secretary of Newtownbreda Baptist Church asking if he could book me to sing and speak at one of their services. I was happy to oblige and we agreed a date. Then he began to talk about a member of his church who was lying in hospital critically ill.

'Perhaps you've heard of him,' he said. 'His name's Gerald Davidson.'

I knew a little of the situation – the death or injury of an RUC colleague is always of concern to another member of the force – but I explained that I did not know Gerald personally.

'Well, perhaps you'd pray for him,' said the secretary. 'Things are not looking good for him.'

He rang off and then I went and fetched Shane and headed out into the fields. It was a dull, gloomy November day – a day that reflected my mood, for all I seemed to be hearing was bad news. It had been a full and hectic week at work – a week, in fact, that had finished only a couple of hours earlier, just before Sunday lunch; the enemy, it seemed, had been busier than usual . . . and now this. It seemed unlikely that Gerald Davidson would pull through.

Shane came padding up to me, a stick that I'd thrown for him hanging jauntily from one side of his mouth and his tail wagging furiously. I stooped and took the stick and with my other hand patted his head.

'Good boy!' I encouraged, and he dropped on to his haunches, looking up at me with his big, round eyes while his tail continued to sweep to and fro on the grass. And in a single moment I suddenly realised all that Shane was saying: 'I love you and I trust you. Hey, isn't life fun!'

I sank to one knee and he offered up his paw for me to shake, so I took it. And then, as though the dog might understand me, I said: 'Shane, this is a crazy world. All this hating and fighting and killing. It's madness. Utter madness. Such inhumanity to man . . .'

But a moment later Shane was away, chasing after a bird that had swooped low over the ground, and I was left alone with my thoughts. I stood up and found myself gazing down into the valley of Belfast where the high-rise flats and the industrial developments jostled shoulder to shoulder in the shadow of the Divis Mountain. Once, many years ago it seemed now, this was my patch – the famous B Division. The Springfield Road, Andersonstown, The Falls . . . Now these difficult areas were in the hands of other officers – men like Gerald Davidson. But at that very moment, Officer Davidson – a devoted husband and the father of two young kiddies – lay in the Victoria Hospital fighting for his life.

The words of the church secretary came to me: 'Pray for Gerald.' And so, standing there in the November gloom with my thoughts still resting on the distant valley, I lifted my heart in prayer.

And then something strange happened. As I visualised Gerald lying there, and as I thought of his young wife visiting him, I felt deeply moved in my spirit, as though I was becoming emotionally involved with two people I'd never even met. And before I knew it there were tears in my eyes.

It was some time later that I learned that Gerald had died about that very time.

I didn't meet Jennie Davidson until the following summer. I was up at Portrush for a week of CPA (Christian Police Association) meetings and I discovered that Jennie and her two children were also attending. I was introduced to her following the Sunday morning service at the local Baptist Church and straightaway my heart went out to her, just as it had on that afternoon that Gerald died. We had a brief chat and I told her that I would like to talk with her some time, thinking that I might share with her what had happened to me on that Sunday afternoon out in the fields as I had started to pray for Gerald. At the time I didn't exactly know why I had felt so deeply for the Davidsons, but later on, when Lily and I had a chance to get to know Jennie better, I began to wonder whether God had drawn us together in this way so that Jennie's story could be shared through the pages of this book.

One of the things which helped point me in this direction was the fact that during the dark hours of heartache and distress following Gerald's death, Jennie had been helped by reading Avril Cummings' experiences in *Hope in 'Bomb City'*. In fact, she told me later, as a result of the help she had derived from the book, she began to recommend it to others and to give copies away to other people whom she believed would benefit from reading the book, including Gerald's police colleagues.

It soon became clear that if Jennie's story was to be told we would need to sit down and talk, and so we fixed a date when we could visit her at home.

It was a glorious summer evening when we set out to drive the few miles to Newtownbreda – a perfect evening for a spin in the car, and for visiting friends. We found the house without difficulty: a neat, red-brick semi in a quiet, tree-lined avenue, away up in one of the hilltop areas of the district. Jennie had been looking out for us and came to the door as we stepped through the gate. She greeted us warmly, her bright eyes betraying nothing of the sadness of her circumstances, and with smiles and cheery chatter she showed us into the lounge – a neat, comfortable room splashed with soft evening sunlight from the large picture window. As we settled into the Tudor style armchairs with their pretty tapestry cushions Lily asked about the children, three-year-old Emma, and Michael, nine.

Jennie smiled. 'They're doing well. Michael's in the other room, watching television. Emma's in bed – asleep, I hope! You know what they're like.'

'Oh, we know!' said Lily, grinning.

We talked on for a while about the kids, both Jennie's and ours, passing the time and getting to know each other better. And yet, as we talked, we were reminded of the reason for our visit because standing on a little table beneath the sunny window-sill was a framed portrait of the husband and father who would never return home again. Beneath the picture, on a stand of its own, was an oblong block bearing a small RUC badge and an inscription. Squinting across the room I could just make out the legend: 'What I do thou knowest not now – but thou shalt know hereafter.' I recognised the words as those of Jesus, recorded in John 13.

Jennie noticed that the block had caught my eye and didn't hesitate to help ease me into the tender area of the tragedy and her loss.

'My Dad had that made for me after Gerald's death,' she explained, fondness and regret meeting in her smile. 'That text had meant a lot to me, ever since we lost our second baby. He only lived a day.'

'Oh, I'm so sorry,' said Lily, and for a moment she and I were silent, both of us momentarily stunned by how much tragedy had struck this young family.

Jennie reached for the block and sat studying it for a moment, slipping in and out of a little reverie. After a short pause she said, 'I can see now that the Lord allowed the baby's death – to help prepare me for losing Gerald.'

She went on to speak with great tenderness of her husband, and yet somehow I became aware that she seemed to have accepted his death as almost inevitable. I asked her if that was how she felt.

'Yes,' she replied without hesitation. 'I believe and accept that Gerald's time had come, and that if he hadn't died the way he did then something else would have happened to him. It was God's time. There's no question of that in my mind.'

As we talked I learned a lot about Jennie and Gerald Davidson. They met when they were both fourteen, but it was another three years before they started going out together. At that time neither had any strong Christian beliefs, but things were to change when, a year later, a friend invited them to attend a gospel service at his church one Sunday evening. Before that service was over both Jennie and Gerald had committed their lives to Christ.

Perhaps this was no surprise as far as Jennie was concerned, for she had been brought up in a Christian home and deep in her heart she knew how much she needed the Saviour. It seemed it was only a matter of time before she gave up resisting his call.

For Gerald it was very different. He had no strong church connections, and the fact that he responded as he did is a testimony to the activity of God's hand preparing the way ahead.

As their faith grew Jennie and Gerald became aware that it was God who had drawn them together, and as this sense of God's direction increased so their love for each other flourished. A year later they married and set up home in Castlereagh. The following year Michael was born, and along with Gerald's new domestic responsibilities came the broader sense of duty to his country. Like so many young men in the province he had reached the point where he could no longer stand back and watch terrorism ravage his homeland, but at the same time he was not prepared to fight back by taking the law into his own hands. He didn't want to give up his work as a motor mechanic, which he enjoyed, so he signed on with the UDR (Ulster Defence Regiment) as a part-time soldier. But this wasn't to last long.

I suppose an outsider would think that a Protestant couple living on a Protestant estate would have nothing to fear from their own community. But even among neighbours one is not necessarily safe in Northern Ireland. The Loyalist groups were quite strong in this estate and on one occasion when they came round collecting for funds Jennie declined to make a donation. The next day a brick came through the window. (Rightly or wrongly, the Davidsons assumed there was a connection.)

A week later Gerald was on patrol at the top of his road when he was stoned by youths from the next street. (This was at a time when the Protestant groups were very active and frustrations were running high – frustrations which were being given vent in open hostility towards the security forces because of their alleged lack of success in dealing with the terrorism of the IRA.) On top of this, Gerald was being threatened by people in the Catholic area where he worked. Naturally concerned for his own safety, he applied to the authorities for a handgun but was refused a permit. With the pressures mounting, and having been in the UDR less than a year, he decided enough was enough and resigned.

But now that he was no longer playing some part in his country's defence the feelings of helplessness and frustration with the enemy began to return. He knew he had to do something – and a few months later, in 1973, he joined the Police Reserve. Things worked out better this time, so much so that after two years in the Reserve Gerald joined the RUC as a regular. It was about this time that the Davidsons also moved house, to Newtownbreda, and with this move Jennie and Gerald finally settled in a church – Newtownbreda Baptist. Until then they had tended to drift from one fellowship to another. Now, at last, their previously erratic lifestyle was levelling out. They were beginning to feel at home. But it wasn't long before something else happened to put strain on their domestic affairs.

'It came in the form of Gerald's first posting,' Jennie told us. 'He was assigned to B Division – one of the toughest areas, as you know, Ben. I used to worry a lot for Gerald's safety, and I was angry, too; angry that his first posting was in such a dangerous area. I felt that for any officer who worked in that district there was a greater risk of injury, or worse, at the hands of the IRA.'

'I know just how you felt,' said Lily. 'I had plenty of anxious moments when Ben was at Springfield Road. It's a really testing time for your faith.'

Jennie nodded. 'It is. And yet deep down I knew that nothing could touch Gerald that was outside of God's will for him, and that was a great comfort. Gradually, though, as we fell into a routine, I felt more and more at peace about the situation, and as it turned out Gerald

28

was very happy at Springfield Road, and there was no way that he wanted to move. He loved working with the people there.'

I glanced at Jennie, a little surprised.

'Jennie,' I said, 'I know from experience how hostile some of the people in that area can be. You're talking about Catholic strongholds – and yet you say Gerald found a certain amount of enjoyment working there?'

Jennie smiled. 'He did. Ben, Gerald knew from working with those people that it was only a minority in that area who were involved in terrorism. Most of them would like to be rid of the terrorists.' She paused for a moment. 'I know it's not what you see on the News, but Gerald made a lot of friends in that area. Of course he came up against a lot of hostility, but he made a lot of friends as well. It was the same when he was transferred to Roden Street. In fact a lot of people who knew Gerald contacted me after his death, and one woman – a Roman Catholic – came all the way from Roden Street to tell me how sorry she and so many of the women there felt about Gerald's death. They wanted nothing to do with terrorism, and I know from what Gerald said that there were a lot of people like that.'

From the beginning Jennie had spoken freely with us, but so far she hadn't touched directly on Gerald's death, so we trod carefully as we approached the subject. But there was no need: she was perfectly at peace about it and didn't hesitate to explain the circumstances surrounding the murder.

'Gerald had taken a week's leave at the end of October to study for the Sergeant's exam which he proposed to take the following March. The weather turned out good that week and we were able to spend a lot of time together as a family. Emma was eighteen months then and this was the first opportunity we'd had to relax as a family for some time.' She paused, smiling reflectively. 'You know, it's wonderful how you can see God's hand

29

in such circumstances. Little evidences of his love. He knew what was going to happen . . . And then, on the Saturday night – the night before it happened – God stepped in again. We'd had visitors that evening and Emma hadn't settled down to sleep very well. Twice I got up to her in the night, but on the third occasion Gerald got up. Now normally he never got up if the children needed attention, but for some reason Gerald got up and took Emma downstairs and gave her a drink and talked to her. Of course, at the time I thought it was strange, but afterwards I realised it was the last time he nursed his little girl.' She glanced at us, her bright eyes smiling at the memory. 'You see, I believe that's the love of God. So compassionate, so loving, so caring – even in the little things.'

The next morning Gerald went to work while Jennie took the children with her to Newtownbreda church. After lunch, with Michael at Sunday School, Jennie was sitting listening to some records when she saw a car draw up outside. A man and a young woman in civilian clothes got out and came to the door and introduced themselves as police officers. They told her that there had been an accident and that Gerald was seriously wounded.

'When I first saw Gerald, in the hospital, I thought he would be all right,' said Jennie. 'He was conscious and knew I was there. But he was on a breathing machine. We knew one of the doctors on the case – a Christian friend – and he told me that probably Gerald would be paralysed, but that their first concern was to get him breathing on his own. But Gerald didn't change and he was kept heavily sedated, and I realised he was very ill. There were a couple of days when he was able to eat and things looked better, but eventually the doctor told me that he would never be able to breathe again on his own.'

I glanced toward the window. The light was fading now, but an orange glow in the sky promised a fine day again tomorrow. I turned to Jennie and spoke softly through the dusk.

'How did you cope?'

She did not hesitate in her reply.

'My faith. I couldn't even have gone to the hospital for those three weeks without prayer and without God's support. Quite often I would sit there by the bed just praying, and at that time I began to realise the true meaning of prayer. But it was the peace I had which got me through it; a peace which I couldn't explain at all. Right from the very moment Gerald died, although his body was lying there, I had this wonderful peace. I knew that this was just an empty shell; that Gerald had already gone, and that he was safe.' She paused, biting her lip. 'I don't mean to make it sound easy, as though my faith took all the hurt away, because it didn't. But Jesus talked about giving us a peace that passes understanding – *his* peace – and that's what I had. His peace enabled me to bear what I had to bear. Sometimes the peace was stronger than at other times, but then sometimes my need was greater than at other times. On the day of the funeral, for example, I felt that I wouldn't even be able to go through the service, but God was with me, and I prayed throughout the service, and he gave me a wonderful peace. Of course, there were many friends with me who were willing and helping me through the ordeal, and I was even able to attend the burial at Lisburn.'

We took a break then. Jennie went and made coffee and for a while we sat talking of lesser things. But inevitably the conversation came round to Gerald again and I reminded Jennie that at that time the murderers were still free. How did she feel towards those men?

'At first, when Gerald was in hospital, I didn't think about them at all. I didn't wonder who had done it, or why. It was only afterwards that I started to think about it, and then I thought that they couldn't have realised what they were doing. There was no hatred. It's strange, but before this happened I had heard other women who had lost their husbands in this way say that they didn't feel any hatred – and I told myself that was a lot of nonsense; that they were bound to feel bitter, bound to hate the people who did this to them. But then when they took Gerald from me I understood. *I* didn't hate them either. Just as Gerald never hated them. He didn't hate the IRA, and he had seen what they could do to people. Sure, he got angry about the situation sometimes, but he never hated anyone. And our children won't be taught to hate anyone, either. We never talked to Michael about the IRA or the Protestant extremists. To him they are just bad men. To this day he doesn't know it was the IRA who killed his Daddy; it was just the bad men. But growing up in Northern Ireland, he'll soon learn about those people, more's the pity.'

I knew that there was one more question begging to be asked of Jennie that night, but I needed time to think and as Jennie refilled my coffee cup I considered what she had just shared with us about the absence of hatred for Gerald's murderers. In the course of my police work I have been involved in investigations into possibly hundreds of murders and as I sat there sipping my coffee I found myself asking whether, realistically, Jennie's attitude could be the right one. I know of many, many people who would disagree with her; people whose response to the murder of a friend or a loved one would be one of hatred and vengeance.

But then it began to dawn on me that that was what I had come to expect; as a result, the opposite view – Jennie's view – came as a surprise. But it shouldn't have, and subsequently, as I have looked for the absence of hatred in those bereaved at the hand of the terrorist, the more I have found it.

Interestingly, for some people, it seems, their refusal to hate the murderer is in itself a form of retaliation. For they have realised that hatred is what the terrorist wants to create – indeed, that it is essential if he is to perpetuate his campaign of violence – and as a result many of those bereaved by the terrorist have refused to give him the satisfaction of knowing that he has succeeded in the psychological aspect of his crime, even if he has achieved his physical goal.

But, of course, the absence of hatred is one thing; the presence of love is something quite different. In order to love, one must first forgive. And here was that final, pressing question. Had Jennie Davidson forgiven the men who murdered her husband?

'I couldn't at first. I didn't hate them, but I couldn't forgive them. I can now, though. It took eighteen months. You see, I believe that there is a sense in which we are all victims of circumstance – "there but for the grace of God go I" – and I am convinced that the majority of people, especially young people, who get involved in terrorism do so simply because of their circumstances, or because their friends are in it, or perhaps because they are intimidated into it. I couldn't always see this, but I was helped by a discussion we had in our church group one Friday morning. Now I realise just how fortunate I am to have been born into a Christian home and brought up in the Christian faith, for I might just as easily have been born to a mother and father who had very different views. And who knows what *I* would have turned out like in those circumstances? Perhaps *I* would be out there throwing stones at soldiers, or even killing policemen.

'But we can't leave it there. Understanding isn't enough; it's only a beginning. We have to tell them that God loves them – that *we* love them – and that they can change. I believe that many of them are prisoners to the belief that, try as they might, they can never change. But that's not true because it's reasoning without the love and the power of God. And I'll tell you this: if *I*

33

was in that situation I'd like to think that somebody would come and tell *me* about that love and that power.'

We sat in silence for a moment, mentally reeling a little from the implications of what Jennie was suggesting, and I had to be sure. I turned to her, a little hesitant, for this went way beyond forgiveness.

'Jennie,' I began slowly, 'would you be willing to tell the men who murdered Gerald that God loves them?'

She hesitated only for a second.

'Yes, I would. And after that it's entirely up to them; it's between God and themselves. Nobody can force them to give up what they are doing, but, yes, I do believe they should have the opportunity to find God's forgiveness and to start their lives afresh – because that's what becoming a Christian means. Jesus said it himself: "You must be born again." How are these people going to change unless someone tells them? And if it comes down to me . . . yes, I'll tell Gerald's murderers that Jesus loves them.'

And that's love in 'Bomb City'.

4: Love thy neighbour

It had been a long, hard winter and now at last spring was here. Only a few days earlier Lily and I had celebrated our wedding anniversary – April 1 – and once we reach that landmark in our year we always begin to look for the buds and shoots in the gardens as a sign that the warmer weather is on its way. This year was no disappointment; in fact, it seemed that the spring flowers and the tree blossoms appeared almost overnight, as though they had been hovering impatiently on the threshold of the new season, anxious to burst into view the moment Mother Nature stirred herself from winter's long slumber.

And talking of slumbering, that's just about how I felt on that gloriously sunny morning as I relaxed in my garden chair out front of our house. The previous day I'd been working late on a case and after a fitful night's sleep I still felt tired. This was Sunday and a little later on we would be heading out to church as a family, but there was no rush and so I closed my eyes and lay back in the sun-lounger, soaking up the gentle warmth of the sun.

I suppose I must have been lying there for some time before the church bells began tolling, their sweet metallic notes drifting across the fields from the next village some two or three miles away. The tune was 'O worship the King, all glorious above' – a hymn which, as I thought about it, I seemed to have known all my life, for the distant notes stirred distant memories . . . faded pictures of grey-flannelled schoolboys belting out those very words in school assembly away back down the years in the little brick schoolhouse in Portadown. I smiled to myself at the memory, but suddenly the pleasant reverie was snatched away by the raucous clattering of an army helicopter whirring overhead. You can never get away from the troubles for long, even on an idyllic Sunday morning.

By the time the chopper had moved on the bells' tune had changed, this time to 'Stand up, stand up for Jesus', and now my thoughts went to Drumcree Parish Church and the Sunday services which punctuated the weeks of my early years . . . and in stark contrast to the April sunshine I remembered the chilling wintry scene as I trudged home from church that Christmas morning in 1957 (an unbelievable quarter of a century ago!) with a new song on my lips. Earlier that year God had spoken to me quite clearly about my need to receive his forgiveness and to commit my life to him, but like so many whom God calls I had resisted . . . But no longer. By his Spirit, God had sown a seed in my heart and I was hungry for him. At the minister's invitation to 'repent of your sins . . . draw near with faith' I responded, stepping out in trust, and stepping into a relationship based on faith in Christ as my Saviour . . . a relationship which has deepened and grown with the years.

I recall that morning with fondness. It was a white Christmas – or, more precisely, a dirty-grey one, the crisp snow having turned to slush in the streets – and on my way to the church that morning I had picked a route along the pavements and dodged beneath the dripping trees, my heart heavy with the need to get my relationship with the Almighty straightened out.

The walk back to the house was very different; the confidence of sins forgiven and the inspiring prospect of a new life in Christ lifted the burden from my soul and in its place I felt the deep and profound peace of God.

I don't recall the physical aspect of that brief journey, however. I suppose I sploshed my way through the slush. But inwardly my feet didn't even touch the ground!

Then someone was calling my name . . . and as I stirred I saw Keri and Clive's bright young faces grinning down at me. Clive was hopping excitedly from one foot to the other.

'Daddy, we're playing high-jumping, and we need a mattress or something to land on.'

'If not a mattress then perhaps an old blanket,' suggested Keri. 'And what about the pillows off your bed? We won't do them any harm; we'll cover them with the blanket.'

I stretched and sat up, smiling. 'Well, I don't think Mummy will take too kindly to you jumping on her best pillows. You'd better go and ask her.'

The problem was solved after a rummage through the loft (the pillow idea did not go down too well!) and soon Keri and Clive emerged triumphant, clutching the mattress from our old carry-cot. And so the kids returned to their game, leaving me to relax once more. But then Shane appeared on the scene with the distinct impression that the high-jump had been erected solely for his benefit, and before I'd had a chance to shut my eyes Keri was calling out for me to come and remove the dog. Now, good dogs obey commands, like 'sit' and 'lie', but Shane was always the reluctant pupil, especially if he could be joining in some fun game. So, after much protesting from the youngsters, up I got to hunt out Shane's favourite ball in order to coax him away from the athletics. So much for a peaceful Sunday morning!

Time was pushing on now, anyway, and soon I had to go indoors to get ready for church. While I stood in front of the wardrobe mirror fixing my tie I heard Lily call out from the living room: 'Oh no! Not again!' She had been listening to the news on the radio and a moment later appeared at the door of the bedroom.

'What's up?' I asked, pulling on my jacket.

'St. T's has been bombed again,' she said, and the frustration showed on her face. 'I don't know – that must be about the twentieth time.'

St. T's is a Roman Catholic chapel about five miles from where we live. It is a small, modest-looking building which evidently meets the needs of the Roman Catholic worshippers in that area. I have never been inside it, but I understand that it is a homely sort of chapel. It also happens to be a frequent target of those wishing to vent their anger towards the Roman Catholic people. I have lost count of the number of times the chapel has been damaged by fire-bombs.

Lily and I know all about St. T's sorry history because along the street from us live friends of ours, Tom and Mary, who worship there. We have known this family for some years and our friendship as neighbours has developed 'over the garden wall' as we have passed by each other's house. Keri is friendly with Anne, Tom and Mary's daughter, and they share many things in common, including a love of music. They attend the same classes each week and Lily and Mary take it in turn to drive them to the tutor's house for piano lessons.

When I was a boy my father taught me that 'no man is bad because of a label'. Now it just so happens that Lily and I have the label 'Protestant'. It is the same label worn by the people who throw fire-bombs at St. T's from time to time. But we would like to think that, despite our label, Tom and Mary do not regard us as guilty of damaging their church. In fact we know they don't. That would be absurd. We are Tom and Mary's friends. We like and respect them, and we believe the feeling to be mutual. Perhaps their regard for us is best summed up in a brief phone call I received from Mary one evening.

'Ben, I don't want to alarm you, but I've just had someone at the door asking if I knew where you lived. It was a man with a brief-case. Now it might be genuine, but I just wanted to let you know.'

That was all. I thanked Mary, put down the phone, and prepared myself for any unwanted visitor. As it turned out the caller was making an innocent enquiry and there was no cause for alarm. But Mary knew only too well that policemen sometimes get shot on their own doorsteps and she didn't want to see that happen to her neighbour and friend. She knows that not all Protestants are bad, even if some do hate her own people enough to try to burn down her church. (In fact Protestants have been among those who have given financial and practical help to assist with the repair of the church.) Equally, I know that not all Catholics are bad people, even if some of them murder my colleagues. Tom and Mary are living proof of that.

But, sadly, far too many people in Ulster, Catholics and Protestants alike, have adopted the 'only-good-Indian-is-a-dead-one' mentality. Frustrated with the continuing violence in their homeland they have allowed the truth to be blurred by bitterness and anger – and the result all too often is another death. Only a week earlier it had fallen to me to interview such a man, a man named Harry. And as we drove to church amid the buds and blossoms that morning I told Lily about him . . .

I got down to Castlereagh Police Office at about six o'clock that evening and found that Harry had been brought in for questioning about an hour earlier. He was suspected of being involved in the murder of two Roman Catholics at a bar in downtown Belfast – a case that we had been working on for some months. The break-through had come in the last couple of days following the discovery of fresh clues . . . and now here was Harry sitting at the table in the interview room, nervously puffing on a cigarette and glancing self-consciously at the watching eye of the security camera suspended from the ceiling in a corner of the room.

I settled myself across the table from the suspect and eased myself into a conversation with him – a conversation which, for the first hour or so, was pretty much one-sided. But eventually he responded, and in the light of the critical new evidence he finally acknowledged his part in the murders.

I leaned forward and set to the task of getting the statement down on paper, and as I did so it became clear that he was ready and willing to talk – not to unburden himself, as is often the case after a confession, but apparently to seek to justify his actions. Evidently he thought he'd done the world a favour by helping to murder some Roman Catholics and wanted me to know it. I told him I wasn't impressed, but that if he wanted to go on I was willing to listen. After all, no man is born a murderer, and if I am to take the gospel of Christ seriously, which I do, I must believe that no man is beyond God's forgiveness. And if Christ is not prepared to abandon the murderer to the rubbish heap then I too must be willing to reach out a hand to even the worst offender.

'Tell me, Harry,' I said, 'how did all this begin?'

He glanced at me. 'How did it begin?'

'Yes,' I said. 'What led up to these murders? I'll wager your parents didn't teach you to hate and kill.'

He held me with his eyes for several seconds more, then glanced down at the table. His fingers found my pen and began toying with it while his thoughts flew away back down the years, or so I guessed. He was silent for a very long time, and at last I said, 'Do you want to tell me about it?'

He did.

Harry was brought up in East Belfast, one of five children born into a Presbyterian family. Through church attendance and what was taught in the home Harry learned the Christian values which for so long have been the vital foundation of our society and he grew up with reverence for God and respect for man. After leaving school he took a job in a shipping office as a junior clerk, and after several years and various promotions he was presented with the opportunity to work abroad. By this time Harry was married and had three children, and with the pressures of living under a terrorist campaign increasing he was glad of the opportunity to get his family away to a more peaceful environment. This posting lasted for five years, after which promotion drew him back to Belfast. And he was happy to return; he had missed his Ulster and welcomed the move with a fresh appreciation and love for the land of his birth.

But then things started to go wrong. The company fell into financial difficulties and redundancies became necessary. Four months later Harry was out of a job. Unable to secure further employment, and having exhausted most of his savings, he was eventually forced to move into a smaller house . . . a move which took him from a fairly exclusive and predominantly Protestant area to a working class locality shared by both sectors of the community. For the first time in his life Harry found himself with Catholic neighbours, and for the first time he found himself being snubbed.

'They didn't trust me,' he said. 'I sensed that from the day we moved in. Our other neighbours told us what they were like; anyway, you could tell they were different. I only ever spoke to them once, but it was obvious they wanted to keep their distance. Then we had a brick through our window one night, and – well, it just had to be that lot – Catholics, I mean – and we just avoided each other after that.'

It was at this time that the terrorist campaign was being stepped up – notably, Harry thought, in his own locality – and with the IRA bent on destroying the country's economy Harry began to associate the loss of his job and his forced move down the social scale with the increased terrorism.

As lawlessness flourished, with more and more turning to violence, and with time on his hands to think, Harry became increasingly frustrated, particularly as he felt that not enough was being done to bring the offenders to justice.

Several weeks later one of Harry's Protestant neighbours – a local shopkeeper – was murdered in cold-blood outside his home. The RUC could find no motive for the killing and came to the conclusion that it was a reprisal for the murder of a Catholic shopkeeper a week earlier.

That same week a civil rights march was held in Belfast. Among the marchers were members of Republican groups, which meant that the rally had to be guarded by the police against reaction from extremist Loyalist groups. In his increasingly unsettled state of mind Harry misread the police presence and found himself asking what sort of society was it that allowed people who were clearly pro-IRA to hold public meetings under the protection of the very law which they were bent on destroying.

Meanwhile, his own personal circumstances continued to deteriorate – he began sliding into debt – and Harry's prejudice slowly turned to bitterness as he began to believe that the law was operating two standards, one for Roman Catholics and one for Protestants, apparently with more protection being afforded to Republicans than Loyalists.

'I asked myself,' said Harry, 'what had happened to the standards we'd grown up with. It seemed that the very fabric of our society was being whipped from under our feet, and that the law which used to govern our world was crumbling before our eyes. Everywhere I looked Protestants were being killed. *My* people were being murdered. And so few of the killers were being caught that I wondered if there was any law left in the land.'

And the more frustrated and disillusioned Harry became with the law of the Crown, the more convinced he became that the only answer was the law of the gun.

Still with no work to go to, and with so much time to kill during the day, Harry found himself drinking in the working men's clubs with other men who followed his line of thinking, and gradually, one thing leading to another, he drifted into the company of the para-military groups. Here were the lads who were willing to put their thoughts into action . . . men who weren't prepared to leave the IRA to the security forces . . . men who were committed to striking back . . . men who could get hold of guns and who weren't afraid to use them.

Amongst these men Harry found a comradeship and a purpose. Like Harry, they were patriots who loved their land; the only difference was that they were prepared to do something about it. What about Harry? they asked. How much did he want to be rid of the IRA? Killing terrorists, they said, wasn't a crime; it was a service to society. It was like stamping out vermin.

Six weeks later two men lay dead in a downtown bar and Harry had a warm revolver in his hand.

In the bare little interview room he threw down my pen and thrust himself backwards on his chair, a smug sort of bitterness blazing in his eyes.

I stared at him. 'I don't think murder is anything to be proud of,' I said. 'Those were innocent men you killed.'

'They were Catholics,' he said.

We pulled into the church car park and I eased the car to a halt. Keri and Clive slid out of their seats and ambled across to where the other young people were sharing a joke, and I turned to face Lily.

'I tell you, love, when I'm faced with a man like that

I wonder whether there's any hope for our country at all.'

She nodded. 'I know, it's awful. If only he hadn't fallen in with the para-militaries . . .'

'Oh, the rot set in long before that,' I said. 'I'll tell you when I think the damage was done: when he refused to have anything to do with his Catholic neighbours.'

'But I thought you said *they* snubbed *him*?'

'That's right,' I said. 'At least, that's what he told me. But it doesn't matter who snubbed who; I dare say they were both suspicious of the other – and why? Because they'd been conditioned into a certain way of thinking . . . expecting the worst and not being willing to give each other a chance to prove that we *can* live together. But sooner or later *someone* has to take the initiative and stretch out a hand of friendship.'

I turned away, glancing out of the car to where our fellow church members were filing into the building, and suddenly I felt an anger rising.

'Just look at us – Protestants, Catholics . . . Republicans, Loyalists . . . you in your small corner and I in mine. I tell you, Lily, it makes me sick!'

I felt her hand on mine and turned to face her. She was wearing a new spring outfit and looked lovely. Smiling across at me she said, 'You know what I think?'

The anger had passed now, and I said, 'What do you think, Lily?'

She said, 'I think we're fortunate to have good neighbours like Tom and Mary.'

And she was right.

5: Thank you for the music

It was the morning of Good Friday and I was looking forward to a long weekend with the family. For the past two years I'd had to work over the Easter holiday, but now we had four empty days ahead of us and we awoke that morning feeling good. It seemed a long time since we'd been able to sit down to a leisurely breakfast as a family, and the extra treat of the traditional hot-cross buns gave our mealtime that special touch. I remember that morning well. There was much laughter, and not a little excitement coming from Keri and Clive as we discussed how we might spend our day. We'd deliberately made no plans, other than to do a few chores around the house and then to head off in the car with a picnic lunch.

'Let's go to Strangford Lough,' was Keri's idea. 'Please, Daddy – it's so pretty there.'

'But there's nothing to do there,' protested Clive. 'Why don't we go to Portrush.'

'Too far,' countered Keri, reaching for the marmalade. 'Shane doesn't want to ride in the car all day, poor thing.'

'Look,' I said, 'Why don't we . . .'

I never finished because the phone summoned me from the table, and when I returned a couple of minutes later three faces were looking up at me, their features poised for disappointment because they'd heard one side of the conversation I'd just had with my sergeant, and they hadn't liked the sound of it.

'Sorry,' I said, and a groan went up from all three of them. 'Maybe this won't take too long . . .'

But it's rare for the questioning of a suspect to be a short process, and as I drove Lily's car down to Castlereagh, leaving the family saloon for their Dad-less outing, I quite expected to be away from home for some hours. I knew the man I was to interview, having questioned him about this particular murder once before, and judging by that encounter I anticipated being engaged with him for the best part of the day. Ah well, there was always tomorrow . . .

He proved to be an awkward customer, more awkward than before because he knew that we were on to him now, and he was wriggling.

After many hours of questioning, however, our suspect finally admitted his part in this crime . . . and then came a pitiful scene: the confession had opened a floodgate through which poured a tide of remorse, spilling into heartache, and soon we had a weeping man on our hands. A man with deep personal problems – problems which now had been compounded by the guilt of murder.

From time to time during the course of my police work I find myself looking across the table at such a man, his life shattered by an act of violence, and how thankful I am that, when the opportunity arises, I can relate the good news that there is one who can rebuild broken lives. Sometimes in these circumstances my mind will go to a verse of Scripture, but on this occasion I felt I should share the words of a song, and as so often happens nowadays that song was one of Marijohn Wilkin's.

Readers of *Hope in 'Bomb City'* may recall that it was one of Marijohn's songs that had come to mind when I had stood on the edge of that bomb crater down in Armagh following the explosion which I referred to in the first chapter of this book. In fact the song which presented itself on this Good Friday morning was the same one that had come to my aid on that August afternoon more than two years before. The song was 'The Mighty Hills of God', and this time, rather than ministering to my own heart, it seemed to be reaching out to the broken man sitting opposite me in the interview room:

> When I need peace like a gentle-flowing river,
> I seek the source and the giver of life;
> For my world-weary soul he will deliver,
> From the turmoil, the struggle and strife.

After the statement had been taken I escorted the suspect down to the cells. Then, having assured him that his family would be notified, I told him I would call in to see him on the following Tuesday (all being well I would be able to enjoy the remainder of the holiday). And then I was away home.

Driving up through Belfast, wondering whether Lily and the kids would have returned home by now, I pressed a music cassette into the player and relaxed to the sounds of one of my favourite albums. But this wasn't simply entertainment. In my job a man meets so much darkness – so much tragedy and misery – that it is important to be able to escape into the light. Gospel music – particularly that which is inspired by the Scriptures or by Christian experience – helps me do that. It provides positive and constructive elements which counteract all the negative and destructive influences which touch my life through dealing daily with murder and terror.

Naturally, some music tapes speak to my soul more effectively than others, and it was not by idle choice that on this occasion, having left behind me yet another depressing case of brutal murder, the cassette now playing was one of those which had proved a continual source of strength to me. Yes, it was a Marijohn Wilkin album, and as the music filled the car, easing me on my journey homeward, I began to reflect on how much this Nashville lady and her music meant to me. So many of her songs semed relevant to my own situation – so much so that I had recorded a number of them myself – and so often they had proved themselves helpful to others, too, as witnessed by events only an hour or two earlier. And then, as I headed up past a mission hall where the previous Sunday I'd sung some of Marijohn's songs to the little gathering there, I recalled how this lady had come into my life . . .

It was a Monday morning in February, 1979. Along with many of my colleagues I was attending a crime conference at Castlereagh Police Office. We'd made a good start on what promised to be a useful programme, dealing swiftly with the preliminaries and getting to grips with the first issue on the agenda, regarding downtown fire-bombs. We were about forty minutes into this discussion when I began to feel unwell. At first I put this down to the stuffiness of the room or to too many late nights – but when the coffee break came around and I tried to stand up I found that I was starting to lose my balance. I sat down again, a little alarmed, now aware that I had lost the feeling in the left side of my head and that my vision was becoming distorted. My colleagues gathered round in concern, and before I knew what was happening I was on my way to see a doctor.

'It seems you may have suffered a minor stroke, Mr. Forde,' was the physician's diagnosis after what seemed an endless examination. He leaned back in his chair, peering at me over the top of his gold-rimmed spectacles, and then pronounced judgement. 'What we need to do now is take things easy for a while. I'm going to recommend that you take two months off work.'

I received the news with mixed feelings. At thirty-nine years of age it is quite alarming to be told that you may have had a stroke, however minor. On the other hand, it appeared that if I took it easy for a few weeks I should make a full recovery. I would miss the game of squash I enjoyed with the lads at regular intervals, but then I wasn't to be confined to bed and there would be plenty of other things to fill my time.

'Don't worry,' said the officer who gave me a lift back home from the doctor's, a wry smile on his face. 'I'm sure your missus'll find you plenty to do. All those little jobs you've been avoiding up until now, for a start!'

Lily was the classic wife. For the first couple of weeks she flapped around me, mollycoddling me like some lame animal the dog had dragged in, refusing to let me do little more than lie prone on the settee all day. But as the weeks passed, and she realised that her husband was not about to expire on the living room carpet, she began manoeuvring me into various activities, both indoors and out, all of which she assured me would be beneficial to my rehabilitation. After five or six weeks, however, the cry was that I was always under her feet, and why didn't I take a trip out to so-and-so . . .

It was while I was away on one of these little excursions, rummaging about in Belfast's Faith Mission Bookshop (a delight at any time!), that I first discovered the music of Marijohn Wilkin. Though it wasn't so much a discovery as an introduction. Edward Douglas, the shop's manager, found me nosing through the latest LPs in the record department and steered me in the direction of an album which he himself had enjoyed, and of which he couldn't speak highly enough. So, armed with my newly purchased record, and with a copy of the Marijohn Wilkin songbook tucked under my arm, I returned home, ensconced myself in the lounge (well out of the way of Lily's feet!), and quickly discovered why Edward had so enthused over this lady's music. Not only was her voice very pleasant on the ear, and the country music sound of the album very agreeable, but the words of the songs came across as spiritually alive. I found I was listening to words which witnessed to a deep, personal experience of both pain and joy. Here, I felt, was someone who had walked in life's shadows as well as in the sunshine of God's love. She was writing and singing from the heart. But more than this, I identified with much of what this lady was saying through her music: her songs were relevant to me in my own situation. Evidently Marijohn Wilkin knew something of the pressures of seeking to live for Christ in a world seemingly gone mad:

Lord, you'll have to talk a little louder,
I can't hear your voice above the noise and strife;
With those televisions blaring and no one even caring
What happens to the other fellow's life.
Lord, you can tell how hard we're trying,
But sometimes it's so hard to hear your will;
With the sirens a-screaming and the multitudes a-teeming,
How I long to hear those words, 'Peace, be still.'

(– from the song 'Speak a Little Louder to Us, Jesus')

Then again she appeared to understand just how weak the human spirit is, and yet how ready God is to reach down to meet us in our trouble:

The faintest flicker of faith, my friend,
Is all he needs to see.
There's no need for words when your thoughts are heard –
He'll find you like he found me.

(– from the song 'Reach Up and Touch God's Hand')

Marijohn seemed to have a special word for me in my role as a Christian policeman, too. Here was I seeking to bring the light of the gospel into the darkness of Ulster's troubles and yet feeling so inadequate. How could *my* small efforts make any real difference? But once more this lady's songs spoke straight into my situation:

Let your light so shine, just enough to light the way –
Not too much to blind, we can't all be Pauls today;
Not with dazzling deeds or with wondrous works you do,
Just enough to let men see the light of love that lives in
you.

(– from the song 'Let Your Light So Shine')

The same song seemed to speak directly about my
encounters with terrorists:

When you see a soul in darkness taking comfort in the
night,
You know he's never seen the Son and he's never known
the light;
Don't blind his eye with dazzling deeds you do,
Just live your life to glorify the Christ who lives in you.

These words were a great encouragement to me because very often it's not possible for me to share my
Saviour through the spoken word – but I can seek to *live*
the gospel each and every day. Another of Marijohn's
songs elaborated upon this:

Lord, let me be a living sermon for thee,
'Cause people would rather see than hear one;
With a smile on my face and my place in the sun,
Doing the things in this world you want done –
Seven days of the week let my every action speak
Louder than anything I could say.
With God as my guide and my eyes to the sky,
Lord, let me be a living sermon for thee.

Lord, let me be an instrument of peace,
Sharing Your love with others.
And where there is strife, Lord, use my life
If you have to – like you sacrificed for your brother;
Not for worldly acclaim, not for personal gain –
Just for the peace I've discovered.
For those who would be greatest or those who are least,
Lord, let me be a living sermon for thee.

(– from the song 'A Living Sermon for Thee')

By the time I was through listening to the album and thumbing through the book of songs I knew I'd found a friend. Clearly the music of Marijohn Wilkin had the touch of the Holy Spirit about it, and having been so blessed by both her words and her melodies I began to wonder whether I might include some of those songs on my next album. First, however, I thought I should write to this talented lady to compliment her and encourage her in her musical ministry. I did so, c/o Word Records in London, adding that I would be pleased to learn how she came to write and record such lovely songs. Her reply, a couple of weeks later, took me by surprise, for I quickly realised that Marijohn Wilkin was something of a VIP in the field of country music. Her letter was headed 'Buckhorn Music Publishing Co., Inc., Nashville, Tennessee' (her own music publishing company), and enclosed was a hardback biography of Marijohn Wilkin.* To my delight the book was inscribed:

To Ben –

This is the story of my life, and
should answer your questions.
In God's love,

Marijohn Wilkin

I devoured the book – and quickly realised how it was that Marijohn was able to write songs that spoke so poignantly to so many human needs: her lyrics sprang from her own experiences of life's dark moments, and from her dicovery that, if we'll only let him, God is there to carry us through.

The death of her father at an early age . . . the strain of helping her heartbroken mother through her loss . . . the death of her own husband after only a few

*Marijohn – Lord, Let Me Leave a Song by Darryl E. Hicks, published by Word Books, Waco, Texas.

months of marriage . . . the break-up of her second marriage and being left to raise a son on her own . . . her struggle against a year-long illness . . . the death of her business partner . . . the loss of her mother . . . the financial difficulties that threatened her business . . . These were the downs which contrasted so starkly with the ups of becoming established as one of Nashville's top songwriters; these were the storm clouds through which Marijohn Wilkin passed before emerging into the sunshine of God's love – a love which opened up a whole new world of music for this Texas lady, for having returned to the faith of her childhood (a faith she had let slip away during her college years) Marijohn found a fresh new source of inspiration for her music, plus the conviction that God wanted her not only to write songs but to sing them too. Thus began a new recording career – a career that got its start with a song that has now become a classic of country gospel music, 'One Day at a Time'.

The more I got to know about Marijohn and the more letters we exchanged (we built up quite a pen-pal relationship!), the more I felt I would love to meet her. And then one day I found out that sometimes dreams do come true . . .

Marijohn was due to visit Ireland on a business trip, and yes, she would come up to Belfast to meet me!

The day of The Visit, planned for February, 1980, drew near amid much excitement and much busyness. A lick of paint was needed here, a spot of polish there – and looking back I think I must have worn poor Lily out.

'Anyone would think the Queen is coming!' she cried. Well, it isn't every day that one of Nashville's living legends drops in for a chat!

And if I had been in any doubt as to just how popular and respected Marijohn Wilkin is then the seemingly endless string of phone calls from Northern Ireland's media people would have put me right. Somehow or other word of Marijohn's visit to my home had got out and suddenly my telephone was a hot-line for all those people wanting me to arrange for the famous lady to be interviewed or to appear on various television or radio programmes. Oh well, it was enjoyable being so popular for a while, even if it *was* on the strength of somebody else's fame!

And so the day arrived. After her engagement in Dublin Marijohn travelled up to Belfast and I arranged to meet her at the studios of Ulster Television where radio and TV personality Gloria Hunniford was to interview her for a television chat show. I was glad of the opportunity to renew an old friendship with Gloria, and of course delighted to meet Marijohn Wilkin in person.

A little later, on our way out of the studios, Marijohn was suddenly surrounded by well-wishers and photographers, as well as by autograph hunters who had rushed to the scene following the live broadcast. Eventually, however, we were on our way home where I introduced Marijohn to the family. Then it was off to a County Down hotel for a special celebration where we relaxed together over dinner, and where we got to know one another. Amazingly, I felt as though I had known Marijohn all my life; I found her so warm, so easy to talk to, so interested in others.

That was a very happy evening, our happiness crowned by the fellowship we shared in our Lord. There was much to say and not enough time to say it. But we were content.

Later, over coffee in a quiet corner of the hotel lounge, I produced a cassette recorder, borrowed from a police colleague, and kept a promise to Ronnie Irvine of Radio Downtown to interview Marijohn for Ronnie's 'Gospel-time' programme. My assignment, of course, was to ask Marijohn about her songs, but having read her book and learned something of the many difficulties she had faced over the years, and how those trying circumstances had eventually drawn her back to her God, I found myself asking Marijohn about more than just her music. This was not simply curiosity. For a long time I had felt that many of her songs were so pertinent to our plight in Ulster – she seemed to have so much to say to us – that it was almost as though she had lived through the Ulster troubles with us. She hadn't, of course, but I was keen to hear from her own lips how she had discovered that it was God who held the key to all her problems.

Between sips of coffee she began, 'Well, Ben – the truth is I think I knew God was the answer all along. But you know how it is; we're stubborn creatures and tend to go our own way. Looking back, I realise that I really didn't have to struggle on through my problems the way I did. I could have handed my hurts to God right from the beginning – and I guess if I'd done that I would have gone into gospel music right from the early days. I believe that was the plan he had for me, anyway; the problem was I took the wrong turning at the crossroads!'

I smiled. 'All we like sheep have gone astray,' I remarked, recalling the words of Isaiah, and Marijohn nodded.

'That's exactly it,' she said. And then she went on to tell me how, over a period of many years, God gently began drawing her back to himself – not by pushing and shoving his way back into her life, but by slowly revealing his love to her, and by showing her that he had the key to unlock and release all the hurt of the past.

'It was a long process. And, you know – something I've discovered: our heavenly Father is very patient. I guess he needs to be! But I also learned that his patience isn't limitless. There came a point when he seemed to say, enough is enough. I knew that he'd been drawing me back bit by bit, but then I reached a point when I couldn't seem to get any closer. I'd been sort of coasting along, but then God seemed to say, "Look, I've given you all this time to return to me, but now I'm not going to wait any longer." Then the Lord just took over, and the last steps of my return were his doing, not mine.'

While I refilled Marijohn's cup she told me that those steps were painful ones. To begin with, her longstanding business partner and friend, Hubert Long, died of cancer. A few months later came another blow when her mother died from a stroke. But instead of reacting bitterly, as she had done when first her father and then her husband had died, she discovered to her surprise that there was a new tenderness in her heart. And this, she knew, meant that God was at work.

But she wasn't out of the woods yet. After her partner's death Marijohn had endeavoured to purchase his share of the company . . . and then found herself with money problems.

'Before I had a chance to sort things out, though,' she continued, 'I had word that my uncle, my only living relative apart from my son, was seriously ill down in Texas. He had lived with my mother, but now he was alone and so I dropped everything and went straight to him.' She paused, smiling reflectively. 'Now that surely was a sign that the Lord was calling me back. It wasn't like me to go off and leave my business affairs in any sort of a fix, but I just felt content to leave the situation in God's hands. The trouble was, as I soon realised, although I was happy to commit my business to the Lord, I wasn't prepared to trust *myself* to him.'

But God was working on that. The few days Marijohn had planned to spend down in Texas stretched into six weeks, and it was during that time, at the bedside of her uncle – a godly Christian man – that Marijohn Wilkin finally returned to her Lord. Having come home to her physical roots, for she was born and raised in Sanger, Texas, she found herself confronted by her spiritual roots . . . and she just couldn't hold out any longer.

She smiled warmly. 'The Lord knew what he was doing. You see, that was where I first learned about Jesus . . . where I first sang duets with my Daddy in church . . . where I first told the Lord I needed him. I was only five years old – and I guess you can't be much of a sinner at that age! – but I knew the Lord was for real, and although there was nothing emotional or dramatic about my conversion, it was sincere. And yes, there was a change; I'd asked Jesus into my life, and no one can be the same after that.

'Well, now I was back in Texas and the Lord brought all these things before me, reminding me of how I'd grown away from him as I'd grown up, because although I had continued to recognise Jesus as my Saviour, he had become less and less my Lord. I could see now that this was where I'd gone wrong. Throughout my life, all the good things that had happened to me had happened when I was walking with God. When I drifted away, things began to slide. While I was close to him I had everything I needed, but as soon as I stepped out of his will everything began to fall apart.'

Apparently the Lord wanted to underline this for Marijohn, for when her uncle had recovered sufficiently to be left on his own she returned to Nashville to find that, in her absence, her financial problems had been compounded by mismanagement of the company. It was crunch time for Marijohn – she couldn't take any more – and she knew she needed help.

'I hadn't been inside a church for years,' she told me as the waitress cleared away our coffee things, 'and not knowing what else to do I turned to the telephone book. The first thing that caught my eye was one of those dial-a-prayer telephone numbers and so I called up. I remember that the pastor's message was on the subject of God's love and I knew more than ever now that this was what I needed, and so I got in my car and drove over.' She laughed shortly. 'All the way there I kept

57

telling myself how crazy this seemed. Here was I in my brand-new Cadillac, all dressed up in my fine clothes – a picture, I suppose, of prosperity and success – and yet I was going knocking on a strange pastor's door asking for help. But ironic or not, I wasn't backing out now!'

After his initial surprise the pastor quickly saw how real was Marijohn's distress, and having spoken with her for some time he recommended that she start to thank God for her problems and to let him handle them. It was sound advice, and after praying with the pastor Marijohn returned home, determined to hand her whole life over to God again. And he was Lord once more.

Back in her comfortable living room, Marijohn confirmed her re-commitment in the way that seemed most appropriate to her. For years she had been writing songs – literally hundreds had flown from her pen and over the years she had been honoured with eight songwriting awards – and now it seemed only natural for her to express her prayer through her music. As it turned out, the resulting prayer-song – 'One Day at a Time' – went around the world, and at the last count it had been recorded by more than two hundred artists. It was a song that I was very fond of myself, and as we sat there, relaxing in the well-sprung hotel armchairs, we reflected on the words together:

I'm only human, I'm just a woman.
Help me believe in what I could be and all that I am.
Show me the stairway I have to climb;
Lord, for my sake, teach me to take one day at a time.

Do you remember when you walked among men?
Well, Jesus, you know, if you're looking below,
That it's worse now than then.
Pushing and shoving, crowding my mind;
So, for my sake, Lord, teach me to take one day at a time.

One day at a time, sweet Jesus,
That's all I'm asking from you.

Just give me the strength to do ev'ry day
What I have to do.
Yesterday's gone, sweet Jesus,
And tomorrow may never be mine.
Lord, help me today, show me the way,
One day at a time.

'Of course, as you know, that was only the beginning, Ben. In the coming days and weeks there followed one song after another. But it wasn't that I'd planned it that way. I'd often find myself talking to the Lord when sitting at the piano, and it just happened that my praise grew into a song. I just felt I had so much to thank God for.'

I smiled. 'And that's a line from another of your songs,' I said. 'One of my favourites.'

You speak to me in a whisper like the gentle, falling snow;
You tell me the things you think I should know;
The secrets of the ages with the seasons' endless flow –
I've got so much, so much to thank you for.

Eternal life you have given me from the never-ending stream,
Even in the dead of winter, the scent of evergreen,
And from the angels in heaven comes a song for me to sing –
I've got so much, so much to thank you for.

I've got so much, so much, so much to thank you for;
A way to walk in this world I've never known before;
Like a good shepherd you've led me right straight to heaven's door –
I've got so much, so much to thank you for.

(– from the song 'I've got So Much to Thank You For')

As the songs flowed, so Marijohn became aware that God did not want her praise to end with the writing of them. She was to sing them, too; in fact she was to record them. At first, she told me, the thought unnerved her a little; she hadn't done any serious singing for some years.

'But God was in charge now and he wouldn't let me get away from the fact that he wanted me back in the recording studio. He even gave me the title of the album we were to produce: *I Have Returned*. That song just about sums up my whole experience in one verse:

I have returned to the God of my childhood,
To the same simple faith as a child I once knew;
Like the prodigal son, I longed for my loved ones,
For the comforts of home and the God I outgrew.

'That really was some recording session,' Marijohn recalled. 'I think it was quite an experience for everyone involved. As one of the guitar pickers remarked afterwards: "That's the first time I ever went into a studio session and felt like I'd been to church!" I remember it as a beautiful time of praise; a unique occasion.'

I remembered reading in her book that Kris Kristofferson wrote the sleeve notes for *I Have Returned* and I asked Marijohn how that had come about. By this time the cassette recorder was rolling and it seemed like here was some good material for Ronnie Irvine's programme.

'That's in the book, too, Ben, if you recall. I'd known Kris for many years – long before he became a big star – and we had always been good friends. Actually, he helped me finish "One Day at a Time" and I wanted to get his reaction to the rest of the songs. He came into the studio when we played back the tapes, and I remember that while we were listening Kris turned away and I knew that he was crying.

'Afterwards he looked at me and said, "Marijohn, I'll be honest – I was afraid that maybe you'd contrived a bunch of gospel songs for this album, but now that I've heard them . . . well, it's so totally honest." It was then I asked Kris if he would write me some sleeve notes and he promised that he would. When they arrived it was my turn to cry. He wrote:

60

"Marijohn,
Sometimes it seems like you've got to go an awful long ways to get back where you started (of course, some of us do get loster than others). You and I have probably shared more grief and glory in the past ten years than we thought we deserved – and, no doubt, we'll continue to do so. But we'll have to go a ways to feel something as good as this album."

'It was short, but my, it was sweet!'

And so was my meeting with Marijohn Wilkin. Shortly after that it was time for us to round off our conversations and to say our goodbyes. How the time had flown! But what memories we would cherish. And as I went back to work next morning – a little bleary-eyed after our late night, I must confess – it was with much thankfulness to God. Thankfulness for the opportunity to become better acquainted with someone I greatly admired, and thankfulness for the feeling I had that, in coming days, the songs of Marijohn Wilkin would somehow prove an even greater help to me, not only in continuing to bring light to some of the dark situations with which I'm faced as a policeman in Northern Ireland, but also in the opportunities I have from time to time to speak a word of comfort into the darkness of those who fall foul of the law and end up with a burden of grief or guilt.

That same day the lady from Nashville flew back home, but within two or three weeks a letter arrived at home bearing the postmark of that famous music city, and there was joy as the family gathered round to discover that as a result of her visit to Ireland Marijohn had written two new songs, one about the 'Emerald Isle' and another which touched much nearer home. At the top of this one, in Marijohn's own hand, were the words: 'To Ben and Lily', and beneath the final line was the signature, Marijohn Wilkin. The song runs like this:

I cry for the dead and I cry for the dying,
I pray for the living, they who keep trying
To establish the peace in a bomb-shelled land
Where fear exceeds the love of a man.

But peace will only fill the hearts
Of the few of those who do their part,
In doing the will of the Father above
Till the whole world believes in him and his love.

I mourn for the mother who took her own life,
But God knows her hurt and the cause of her strife,
And I thought of another standing small in a crowd.
As she heard her son's voice from the cross cry aloud –
forgive them.

Jesus warned us that he hadn't come to bring peace;
The world wasn't ready for the fighting to cease.
He said there'll be war and rumours of war
Till we all claim our sonship and know who we are.

And peace will only fill the hearts
Of the few of those who do their part,
In doing the will of the Father above
Till the whole world believes in him and his love.

That too is love in 'Bomb City' . . . flowing all the
way from Nashville.

6: Surprised by love

Love, like a flower garden, has many colours and complexions. Its fragrances are varied, too. But they are all sweet. And they never mean more than when they take us by surprise. Step into a house where the air hangs thick with the heady aroma of hyacinths . . . or turn a corner in a country lane to set eyes upon a field of scarlet poppies, glorious in the summer sun . . .

Thus love comes to us, ever welcome, but never more precious than when we stumble upon it, or when it arrives, unannounced and shining, on our doorstep.

The love which I find in 'Bomb City' often comes to me like that – when I'm not expecting it, and often from an unlikely source.

One Sunday I heard a pastor say from his pulpit that love can grow almost anywhere, but that it never thrives better than when it springs from furrowed ground. I've thought about that often, and certainly it is true as far as 'Bomb City' is concerned. It seems that love-seeds, like any other kind, have difficulty in taking root in solid, undisturbed ground. But break up the soil a bit and watch those shoots appear.

Adversity makes a good plough. Though unwelcome, it effectively churns the ground, and whether we feel the cutting edge of personal trial or are moved by the harrowing plight of others we can be sure that, sooner or later, something will grow in our hearts. Sadly, and all too often, it's the bindweed of bitterness that flourishes in the newly-scarred ground. But just now and then another, sweeter crop will rise up . . .

About a year ago two people touched my life with love in fresh, unexpected ways, and they did so within the space of a few summer weeks. The first episode began when Alfie, our office manager, stopped me in the corridor of police headquarters one Thursday morning.

'Hey, Ben, I've been wanting a word with you.'

'What is it, Alfie? You're not after money?' I ribbed.

He laughed shortly. 'No, I've a message for you. Did I tell you I have an aunt up in Ballymoney? Well, she has a lady living nearby who'd like to get in touch with you. Lady by the name of Jean Graham. Apparently she's read your book and is eager to talk to you. If possible, she'd like to meet you, so my aunt says, or at least speak with you on the phone. I believe she's house-bound to some degree. Come on into the office; I've got her address somewhere.'

I drove home that evening with the details in my pocket and a mental note tucked away in my mind to ring this lady when I had a spare moment. Since the publication of *Hope in 'Bomb City'* I had received many kind letters from people who had read the book, a number of them expressing their appreciation of something they'd read and which had been of help to them. I'm always glad to receive such letters, and I'm thrilled to know that God is using something of my own experiences to assist others. Time permitting, I seek to answer every letter, but sometimes a reply has to wait, and as I turned the last corner on my journey homeward that evening I could think of a dozen little tasks which would have to be attended to before I could get around to that phone call.

But it seems I'd got my priorities wrong. As I settled down for my tea with Lily a voice from somewhere said, 'Phone Jean Graham.' I ignored it and got stuck into my ham salad.

After the meal I went out into the garage to tinker with the lawn-mower which had been misbehaving now for some weeks, and then there was a puncture to fix on Clive's bike. I'd just got the innertube out when I heard that voice again.

'Ring Jean Graham.'

But Clive had planned an outing with his friends tomorrow and he would be needing the bike.

Half an hour later I stood watching as Clive pedalled gleefully up and down the road on his newly inflated machine, and then it was indoors to sort out some bills. But I didn't get round to writing the cheques.

'Ring Jean Graham.'

I stopped, put down my pen, and cast my thoughts heavenward. 'Lord, are you trying to tell me something?'

There was a loud silence, and I could almost hear the Almighty breathe, 'At last!'

A minute or two later a phone was ringing somewhere in Ballymoney. Then a woman's voice gave the number and I was saying: 'Oh, good evening – this is Ben Forde; could I speak to Jean Graham?'

There was then some delay because apparently Jean was in bed, not feeling too well, but down the line I could hear excited voices somewhere in the distance and after a certain amount of commotion (apparently while the phone was linked up to the bedroom) an unexpectedly bright and bubbly voice came on the line.

'Hello, Ben – this is Jean!'

Strange, this lady didn't sound ill to me! But at that point I wasn't aware of just how irrepressible a lady Miss Jean Graham was. Ill or not, she was excited about what God was doing in her life and in the lives of others.

'And your book, Ben – it's been such a blessing. I keep turning back to it to read wee bits again, and it's wonderful how my Lord speaks to me through its pages. I tell you, Ben – God has his hand on that book. Why, it's been used all over the place. In fact I've lost count of how many copies I've given away!'

Given away? Was Jean Graham well-to-do? Who was paying for the books she was giving away?

She laughed shortly. 'Oh, my Lord takes care of that. Money's no object to him. One pound or a million – he can supply all my needs. It's getting the word out that matters – reaching the people who need my Saviour.'

And thus, in this mildly intoxicating vein, our conversation flowed on until, almost to my surprise, I found myself saying, 'Jean, when can I come and see you?' For here, I knew, was no average Christian. This lady was excited about her faith – no, about her Jesus! – and she wanted the whole world to know. She was not a young person, that was clear, and neither was she enjoying good health (she was, she told me, confined to the house most of the time), but she had something that clearly wasn't cramped by lack of youth or fitness. Something that couldn't be held in by four walls. Her body might have been confined to a bed or a chair, but clearly her spirit was flying.

'Come as soon as you like,' was Jean's open invitation, and sitting there with the mouthpiece hooked under my chin I began flicking through my diary to see when I would be able to get up north. It didn't look good; there were very few blanks in the next few weeks, and apparently none of my engagements would take me anywhere near Ballymoney. But then, just as I'd almost resigned myself to putting off our meeting for the best part of a month, I noticed an alteration I'd made to an engagement the following Tuesday evening. Why, I'd clean forgotten about that one! Yes, I was due to sing at a youth meeting at a little church between Coleraine and Limavady. I'd have to pass through Ballymoney on my way. Perfect.

'Look, Jean,' I said, 'I could manage to slip in to see you early next week . . .'

After I'd replaced the receiver I jotted a little note in

my diary, and as I did so I felt a sudden burst of expectancy. On the face of it, it seemed quite irrational – but I knew something good was going to come out of my meeting with Jean Graham, not least because of that voice which had persisted in urging me to pick up the phone. Tuesday was a day to look forward to.

It was about six-thirty when the car rolled to a halt outside the little prefabricated bungalow. I climbed out, a bundle of books tucked under my arm, and went up to the door. It opened almost immediately and after a preliminary exchange of greetings with Jean's mother and sister I was shown into a little bedroom at the back of the house.

'Ben!'

I recognised the voice immediately, but for a moment I had a job reconciling it with the frail, white-haired person who beamed up at me from her bed. I had understood that Jean was in her early forties – my own age – but evidently years of suffering had taken their toll. Except for the eyes. The eyes were bright, unclouded, piercing.

'I brought you some books,' I said, off-loading my bundle on to a bedside table. 'Some more for you to give away!'

The eyes flashed excitedly, like a little girl at her birthday party.

'Why, Ben, there's another answer to prayer – I sent the last one out this morning. Come and sit beside me.'

I pulled up a chair, a very low chair, and suddenly found myself looking up at Jean as she sat propped against her pillows. Appropriate? I mused. But then the thought was nudged away by the need for words.

'Tell me, Jean, who do you send the books to?'

'Oh, all sorts of people,' she replied. 'Whoever the Lord tells me to send them to. Different books for different people, you see.'

I nodded. 'You've other books, then?'

'Books, tracts, poems, Scripture verses . . . I've got all sorts of wee things that I send to the dear people God lays on my heart.' She smiled widely. 'Here, let me show you something.'

She leaned over and pulled a large cardboard box from her cupboard on the other side of the bed and placed it squarely on her lap. Her long, slender fingers went quickly to the contents – envelopes, letters, folders – and her face lighted up like a queen sorting through her jewels.

'These,' she said with almost palpable pride, 'are my letters. My lovely, God-given letters.'

And God-given they were. They were replies from some of the people to whom Jean had written with a tract or a book or a poem; people, she said, whom God had singled out for her to write to with a word of encouragement or comfort – 'But mostly just to share my Jesus.' There were letters from widows, letters from old people, letters from youngsters . . . letters from around the world, from missionaries and from presidents . . . letters from every strata of society, from plain people to politicians, from rogues to royalty. In all, she said, she writes regularly to scores of people, including many prisoners.

I grinned. 'It's a great encouragement to hear you talking like that, Jean. You know, many people would dismiss the prisoners as beyond hope, but like you I believe we need to extend a hand of friendship to them. I realise that some of them are hard-bitten, evil men who have deliberately chosen the path of violence, but there are many others who truly regret their deeds and would wish to make amends. As opportunity permits, I believe we must reach out to those people.' Jean nodded, and I went on: 'Do you find you get a good response to your letters?'

She smiled. 'I almost always receive a reply, Ben. So many people appreciate the fact that someone has thought of them in their difficulty. And their letters mean so much to me, too. In fact I just live for my letters now.'

Jean's letter-writing ministry, I learned, began about ten years ago, in 1972.

'I lost two aunts who were very dear to me, and through that the Lord burdened me for the bereaved. It didn't matter who they were or what their background was; if I heard of anyone bereaved or read about them in the newspaper I would write to tell them that God loved them. I would tell them of the wonderful things he had done for me and try to show them from the Scriptures what he could do for them, too.' She turned to me. 'Ben, you and I know something of God's love for us, but there are millions of people out there who've never heard, and we have to tell them . . .'

I fell silent for a moment, gazing out through the net-hung window into the sunlit garden beyond. It was a glorious June day, and I was acutely aware that Jean was unable to enjoy it. I glanced at her again.

'Jean,' I said, 'here you are laid up in bed on a beautiful day such as this and you're talking about the love of God. But I can think of plenty of people who would say that if God loved you he wouldn't let you suffer like this.'

She laughed shortly and turned to me, beaming. 'Ben, it's *because* he loves me that I'm like this. You know, when I was a wee girl I was as fit as a flea. Oh, I was a Christian, but I wasn't living for my Lord. I was selfish, living just for me. But God, in his wisdom, knew that if ever I was to receive all that he has for me I would need to listen to him and learn from him. And so, because he loved me, he laid me aside.'

Jean noticed the flicker of my eyebrows and smiled.

'That's right, he laid me aside. At fourteen I was struck down with polio. The Lord took away my sight, my hearing, my speech, and the use of my limbs. But there in my darkness he spoke to me. He said, "You're on your back now, Jean, and the only way you can look is up." And, Ben, as I looked up to him so he brought before me the details of the years I had wasted as a young Christian.'

She paused, turning to gaze out of the window, her eyes resting on the tranquil garden scene as her thoughts flew back down the vista of the years to gather her memories. And when she spoke again there was a new edge to her words . . . a new emotion.

'Oh, I shed many tears over those wasted years. God showed me that not only had I lost my *physical* hearing but that in my *heart* I had stopped listening for him. He showed me that my spiritual sight had been impaired, too. No longer was I looking for the Lord's return, and that was something else he needed lovingly to teach me.

'So that was a great time of learning and of tremendous blessing. I know some people don't understand when I say that, but, you see, it was during that time that the Lord drew so very close to me – closer than I could touch. And I was a different person from then on'

For a long time, Jean told me, her illness kept her in hospital, confined to an iron lung. Apparently her condition was critical and on one occasion the doctors feared for her life and summoned her parents to her bedside in the early hours of one morning. And yet she was to make a remarkable recovery.

'You see,' she went on, 'God had a plan for my life. But I had a lot to learn yet, and several years later, in 1972, he laid me aside again – and once more I was paralysed . . . couldn't move, couldn't see, speak, or hear. It really was a strange experience: lying there on my bed, knowing nothing of the outside world. It was like being stranded in a wilderness. And yet I knew that God had his hand on me and that he had allowed me to be struck down again in order to do something for me or to teach me something.'

'And did you feel sure you would recover again?' My voice sounded strangely thin in that hushed room.

'I did,' she said, quite firmly. 'You see, I was very conscious of the fact that he had work for me to do . . . and besides, the Lord kept bringing Jonah to my mind and somehow I knew that just as Jonah was freed from the darkness of the fish's belly after three days, so I too would be delivered from my darkness in the Lord's time.'

As she lay there during those distant months, shut off from the world and shut in with the Lord, Jean could do little but pray.

'And through that,' she said, 'God gave me a great love for people . . . for that was what I needed to learn. And as my love for people grew so I prayed: "Lord, if you raise me from this bed, paralysed as I am, and give me back my speech and sight, and return to me the power of my hands, I'll tell it to the ends of the earth; I'll write to the farthest corners of the globe to glorify your name. And that prayer was answered!'

She turned to me, a gentle radiance in her eyes.

'I still have my moments of weakness, like now. But, Ben, I've learned that the body is of limited importance; it's only God's temporary arrangement. We can receive his love in whatever state we are physically . . . and we can pray, too, regardless of our weaknesses.'

And then she said: 'That's why I wanted to meet you, Ben. To tell you that God has laid you mightily on my heart. He wants me to pray for you – for your protection, and for your blessing. For that book of yours is powerful and God's going to use it more and more, of that I'm sure. And I just know that he has other things that he wants you to do . . . and for that you're going to need prayer. What do you say?'

I smiled. 'What *can* I say? Jean, I appreciate your sharing with me today – and yes, I'd love for you to pray for me – but only on one condition: that you let me pray for you.'

'Oh, I just love people praying for me, Ben. So it's a deal.' And then she said, 'Now you'll be wanting a cup of tea before you go.'

The plough, it seemed to me, had cut deep into Jean's heart in preparation for the beautiful crop of love that was to grow there in the coming years, and from which I was to benefit. Similarly, the love which came my way from 11-year-old Stephen sprang from adversity. Not his own, mind you: the love-seeds that took root in this young boy's life were carried there by the storm-winds of someone else's tragedy.

It began in August. There were some smiling faces to be found around our home on that Wednesday because next day we would be leaving for a family holiday up on the Antrim coast. I would be tying in our visit to Portrush with a series of CPA holiday meetings, the weather forecast indicated uninterrupted sunshine, and we would be meeting up with many old friends. All in all, it promised to be an enjoyable week's break.

But then the six o'clock news stole our smiles.

'In the Lisburn area a search is going on for a nine-year-old girl, Jennifer Cardy, who has not been seen since leaving her home to play this morning. Police fear that she may have been abducted.'

'Dear God . . .'

I had just arrived home and stepped into the house to hear Lily utter this plea as she stood in the doorway of the lounge, staring in shocked horror at the television set. She turned to me, all colour fading from her face.

'Ben! Wee Jennifer Cardy's gone missing . . .'

Then she looked down at the small dress she stood clutching in her hands, and said again, 'Oh, dear God . . .'

We knew the Cardy family well. They were members

of our church and from time to time we would also meet them at social functions. Lily and Jennifer's mother, Pat, got on well together, and only the previous day Pat had phoned to say that Jennifer was going on a children's camping holiday and that she needed to borrow a fancy dress. Was there any chance that Lily would be able to dig out something suitable from the collection of costumes she had gathered over the years from her work with the Girls Brigade? The dress Lily now stood holding was the one she had chosen for young Jennifer. She had washed it earlier in the day and had been in the middle of ironing it when she went through to snatch a look at the TV news headlines. Pat had arranged to call in and pick up the dress the next morning. She never came.

We know that we were not alone in praying for Jennifer's safety that evening. This sort of thing does not happen very often in Northern Ireland, thank God, and when it does occur it is always deeply shocking. Our hearts went out to Pat and Andrew and their family, and that teatime, as we sat down for our family meal, the usual pre-holiday excitement was notably absent.

The following morning there was still no news of Jennifer's whereabouts and our fears for her safety grew. And as we took off in the car for Portrush it was beneath a cloud. There was enjoyment, of course, in getting away for a break and in renewing old friendships in a holiday atmosphere, but Jennifer's disappearance was very much on people's minds and we found ourselves making sure that we were not too far from a radio when a news bulletin was due. Not that we were inclined to wander any distance from our accommodation or cars, anyway, for the promised sunshine never arrived – in fact rain settled in from the outset of our week – and when we did venture outside it was always in the company of either an umbrella or plastic mac.

Under these circumstances the CPA's morning and evening meetings, held in the local Presbyterian Church, were even more welcome than usual. And here, as we gathered together in prayer – probably a thousand or more of us at each meeting – we were more conscious than ever of that other cloud: the suffering of the Cardy family as they waited in torment for news of their little girl.

As the days dragged on, and still there was no word of Jennifer, so our hearts grew more restless . . . and the more we cried out to our God to intervene.

The spirit of our longing was captured on the Tuesday morning when Bible teacher Derick Bingham brought before us a text from Isaiah: 'Comfort ye, O comfort ye my people.'

'We are living in a time of much evil,' Derick reminded us, 'and surely our need of God's comfort has never been more keenly felt than today . . .'

His word, of course, applied to all of us, but I'm sure I wasn't alone when, on that grey afternoon, my thoughts went to a little white bungalow that we had seen repeatedly on the television news over the past six days . . . the home of Pat and Andrew Cardy. If God's comfort was needed anywhere at this time it was in the hearts of that family. And, as it turned out, it was going to be needed in increasing measure over the coming days.

The news came through on the six o'clock bulletin. Jennifer's young body had been recovered from a lake a few miles from her home.

In an instant the cloud of gloom that had menaced us for six days darkened to despair and rained its agony upon us.

I was stunned. In the course of my work I see too much murder and grief. And now, on top of it all, this cruel blow with the death of an innocent wee girl.

Oh, God . . . WHY?

I was not alone in my grief. Many tears were flowing as, minutes later, we gathered for the evening's pre-meeting prayer time, and together our hearts went out to Jennifer's family as we lifted them to their loving heavenly Father . . . the 'God of all comfort'.

I thought of the songs I had arranged to sing at this meeting . . . and somehow they now seemed empty, irrelevant. Whatever would I do? And even as I was asking the question I knew the answer. My plans would have to be abandoned; the songs would have to be changed.

And so that night I found myself turning once again to the message of 'The Mighty Hills of God': 'When I need peace like a gentle-flowing river . . .' And then, with our thoughts already running ahead to that sweet reunion that God has promised those who love him: 'Will the Circle be Unbroken?'

Our speaker that night was Stan Wright, Assistant Secretary of the CPA, and although I don't recall the theme of his message I do remember that he made no prolonged appeal at its close. I particularly remember this because I know I was surprised to look up during the closing hymn to see a young, fair-haired lad moving slowly and steadily past me towards the front of the church. There he stopped, head bowed in silent conse-cration. I know how lonely it can be out there at the front of a big church, and so as I was in the front row I stepped across to the boy's side where he glanced up at me and we exchanged a small smile of understanding. I was a few years older than this young fellow when I committed my own life to Christ, and I know how glad I was that I wasn't alone when I went forward to the communion rail that Christmas morning and uttered my vow of commitment in the words of the old hymn:

Come into my heart, Lord Jesus.
Come in today, Come in to stay,
Come into my heart, Lord Jesus.

And these were the words I shared with young Stephen when, a few minutes later, he and I sat in the minister's office talking of the need each of us has to be at peace with God. Stephen also spoke of how he had been moved by the tragedy of wee Jennifer Cardy . . . a tragedy which perhaps had spoken to his heart more eloquently than any sermon ever could. And here he was, aware of his need of the Saviour, and ready to commit his young life to God.

Later that night, when we were sitting reading in our room before turning in, Lily looked across at me with what must have been her first trace of a smile since we'd received the distressing news that evening.

'What's on your mind?' I asked.

She closed her Bible and glanced up at me. 'Ben, I was desperately sad when I heard about Jennifer – and I still am – but I was just thinking of what Jesus said about the grain of wheat falling into the ground and dying so that there could be many more grains.'

I looked at her, eager to hear more, for I could see from the light in her eyes that she had caught hold of one of God's truths.

'Go on,' I said.

'Well, it's just that – that I know Jennifer's death is precious in God's sight, and that he won't let it be wasted.'

I nodded. 'I think young Stephen is proof of that.'

It was about a month later that I received a letter from Stephen, and although he did not mention Jennifer I was very aware as I read his words that Lily's Scripture had indeed begun to be fulfilled. In the darkness of that wee girl's death a seed of light had been planted, and here was the promise of a bountiful crop.

Stephen wrote:

Dear Ben,

I apologise for not writing sooner, but I have been so busy – but not so busy that I don't have time to pray and read my Bible, as I know I need to.

Ben, I feel so proud to be able to call you my friend; it really means a lot. That night in August I will never forget as long as I live. My Mum cried, my Dad had been praying for this a long time, and now it really happened. I feel glad to have Christian parents, and a sister called Barbara.

I have a lot to live up to, but I know my family are praying for me, and I hope so are you. I know my family are praying for Mr. and Mrs. Ben Forde and family, plus your friends in the RUC. I pray that God will walk very closely with you as you face danger each and every hour.

And then, once more, I was surprised by love. It was as though I had turned that corner and here was a field of scarlet poppies, glorious in the summer sun.

Until I hear from you again take care and God bless. Try to remember a small boy watching and listening to the TV news each night, hoping and praying that he *won't* hear his friend's name mentioned.

I am the boy, Ben. You are the friend.

Stephen.

7: Memory is the key

The last thing I had in mind that Tuesday morning was a trip down Memory Lane, but any man who returns to the town of his boyhood after a decade or more must, I suppose, expect to stir a few ghosts. Not that I hadn't seen Portadown for all those years: now and then I had passed through its familiar streets in the course of my work. But an awful lot of water had flown under the town's bridge since I'd last made anything other than a flying visit to this quiet place.

Ironically, there had been nothing quiet about the event which drew me back to the old town now. The IRA had planted a bomb under the car of a Portadown man named Jim Wright, and when he turned the ignition key that black July morning back in 1979 the vibration detonated the explosives, killing him instantly.

I had known Jim only a few short years, but I liked him a great deal and felt a deep respect for him. He was a fine Christian man; a keen member of the Salvation Army. Our association, primarily, was based on two mutual interests: singing (like myself, Jim had made a number of gospel records) and policing. When I first met him he was a member of the RUC Reserve, but he later resigned. His resignation, however, did not signal his removal from the terrorists' murder list. As far as they were concerned he was still an enemy. And at 8.15 one morning they made sure that he would never help the security forces again.

When I heard the news I determined to visit Jim's widow, and today seemed a good day for it. I'd had one or two inquiries to make on the outskirts of Portadown that morning, and having completed my business much sooner than expected I headed on into the town in the hope that I would find Mrs. Wright at home. But as I drove through I was distracted by a sign which reminded me of another priority: 'Barber Shop.' I was due in court later on that afternoon and badly needed a haircut. Should I stop now and go on to Mrs. Wright's a little later, or make the visit first and hope that I could leave in good time to get a trim before heading back to Belfast?

Five minutes later I was sitting beneath the scissors, exchanging memories with the barber. Clearly he was enjoying his reminiscing. The problem was, the more he talked the more he chopped, and I ended up with a short-back-and-sides. I knew I shouldn't have started talking about my schooldays! Perhaps I'd stirred him up by recalling that in that far-off age I could get a scalping – er, trim – for just ninepence.

Ah well, if the style hadn't changed the price had made up for it. Perhaps, I mused, there was a charge for the local history lesson.

I stepped out into the street, a sudden gust of January wind nipping at my newly exposed ears, and pushed on to Mrs. Wright's, only to be told by a neighbour that she wasn't at home. Apparently she had taken a job at the local school (where the young Ben Forde menaced his tutors for the best part of nine years!), and it was there that I found her sitting behind a typewriter, doing letters for the Head.

We sat talking about Jim for a while . . . about how she was coping . . . and about her daughter, Ann, who had been injured when about to get into her Dad's car that morning when the bomb exploded.

And then, quite suddenly, she said: 'Would you like

to see round the school?' And I could sense the memories just crowding at the door . . .

It's funny how a place you frequented as a child seems so much smaller when you return, fully grown. I hadn't been inside the old school since the day I'd left it 27 years ago, but it seemed that little had changed. Still the same echoing corridors . . . the same high windows and painted brick walls . . . the same solid wooden doors . . . and – why yes, that same unique 'school smell': a bitter-sweet cocktail of floor polish and ink. Or was that my imagination? Surely the quaint old ink-well (a source of much mischief for anything in short trousers!) was redundant in the computer age?

And then you could have blown me over with a feather! Stepping from one of the classrooms, as if emerging from a time machine, was Old Bisto – er, I mean Mr. Best! I couldn't believe it: one of my old teachers! Still here after 27 years – just as I'd remembered him, except, perhaps, that there were a few flecks of white in his fairish hair (or was it chalk-dust?).

His gaze met mine as I stepped towards him down the ringing corridor, and almost immediately his eyes flashed in recognition.

'Good heavens!' he spluttered. 'Ben Forde.'

'Mr. Best,' I said limply, my mind grappling with the unnerving implications of instant identification after more than a quarter of a century. Surely I'd changed? And then, as I ran my fingers back through my hair in mild dismay, I remembered the barber. I could have strangled him!

'Fancy you remembering me,' I muttered in defence, just managing to smother an automatic 'Sir'.

'I'll never forget you!' he returned – and beamed at me. 'In all my years as a teacher I've only ever had to send one boy off the football pitch, and that was you.'

I gulped, guiltily, and felt the defence of the years crumbling around me.

'Don't know what came over you that day,' he went on. 'Normally you were a good humoured type – ace footballer, too!' he added with a sudden flash of pride. 'But that day – do you remember it? – you went berserk. Kicked another lad black and blue. Had no choice but to send you off.'

'He must have got between me and the goal,' I chuckled. 'I took my football very seriously, Sir.' (There – I'd said it!)

He drew his shoulders back and glanced down his nose at me. But there was a twinkle in his eye as he said: 'Ye-es . . . about the only subject you did take seriously, if I remember rightly.' And then, with a certain amount of triumph: 'Still, we won the Cup a good few times, eh? My word, we had a cracking team in those days . . .'

He let the memory linger for a moment or two, and then suddenly he shot his arm up and glanced at his watch.

'Look, I'd better dash,' he said, 'but get Mrs. Wright to show you the old team photos. You'll spot yourself somewhere. Nice meeting you, Ben.' And then he strode off and vanished through another doorway . . . back into the time-machine.

I turned to Mrs. Wright, shaking my head in amazement.

'After all these years . . .' I said.

She smiled at me. 'Come on, I'll show you those photographs.'

We walked down the corridor, round the corner – and there it was: a veritable Hall of Fame . . . or Rogues' Gallery, depending on your viewpoint. Neatly framed and newly polished, the pictures clung to the shining wall in an orderly and obedient row: moments in time, fragmented and frozen, and ever so proud. A silent history which spoke volumes to those who knew.

'There's my son,' said Mrs. Wright, a faint tremble of pride in her voice, and I thought she was pointing to one of the schoolboys. 'He used to teach here, before he went into the Salvation Army full time.' Then she paused and a distant smile crept into her voice as she said: 'He always wanted to follow his father into the Army, you know.'

In silence we moved slowly down the line, glancing at some prints and pausing at others. Yes, there was my team – and, my goodness, what a bunch we were! I chuckled to myself at the old faces . . . the old style . . . the old haircut (enough said about the haircut!).

'I do believe that's you there, Ben –'

Yes, that was me on the extreme left, a grim sort of victory carved on my features, and a chest so proud I was almost bursting out of my striped jersey.

Mrs. Wright laughed. 'Looks like you could have lost some weight,' she said, dashing my dream.

'My mother always said I was big-boned,' I replied meekly.

Then another voice joined in: a booming voice that exploded from one of the classrooms.

'Get out, boy! GET OUT!'

And although the voice was unfamiliar I recognised the message and shrank away as though it was meant for me. I remember it so well because the teacher who once barked those words at the young Ben Forde was the only one who had ever taken an obvious dislike to me, and he showed it very clearly one afternoon when I asked to be excused. His face is but a memory now, but his immortal words will remain engraved upon my mind for ever:

'Get out!' he cried. 'Get out – and kindly pull the chain on yourself and don't come back!'

We ventured on, peeping back down the corridors of time, the memories rushing at me at every turn. But the hour was pressing on and I knew I ought to be moving. At the main entrance I thanked Mrs. Wright for the tour and headed back to the car, but I should have known better than to think that I could stir the ghosts of my childhood and then leave without acknowledging each one. And at the school gates another memory leapt out at me.

In my later years at school I was always one of the first boys to arrive in the morning, not because I was keen to learn, but because if we helped the caretaker get the crates of milk round to the classrooms early enough he would let us take a football down to the playing field for a pre-school kick-about. What bliss!

And then, as I glanced back at the railings, I remembered how we used to gain entry to the premises on those occasions. The gates were never open that early in the morning (once the milk had been delivered the caretaker would lock them again) and so we squeezed in through the railings. There was a bent one somewhere, and – yes, there it was, to the right of the gate. I stopped and studied the space for a moment. Was I *really* once that small (regardless of Mrs. Wright's withering joke)? One thing was for sure: I would never pass that way again. And then, for no good reason, and to my regret, I suddenly thought of Noel, my super-slim colleague – he of the non-existent waist and the slimline trousers – and I had a horrible feeling that *he* would be able to leap through those railings with space to spare.

'Don't torment yourself, Ben,' I muttered under my breath, and climbed into the car. Thankfully, it was at that moment that another memory came to my rescue . . . a little incident to which these same school gates had been witness.

It happened about a month after I'd left school. I'd started work as a messenger boy for the local newspaper, the *Portadown News*, and entrusted to me in my lofty position was a wonderful machine known as a messenger bike. This had all the usual amenities, but its star attraction was a very big box mounted over the front wheel. As a rule this box was for the transportation of packages, but after office hours it often doubled as the conveyor of my team's football gear. (I was still football mad and was into my boots at every opportunity.) On this occasion the famous box was slightly crowded because along with the team strip it contained the not altogether small shape of my pal 'Petesy' McCann. Peter and I were on our way to a match and we were late. The sensible thing to do, it seemed to us, was to use the bike: me on the saddle and Peter in the box.

This arrangement, though a little wobbly on corners, worked very well. Unfortunately the local policeman did not share our enthusiasm, a fact which he expressed in amazingly colourful terms when he stopped us outside the school gates and booked us for riding two on a bike.

'My Dad'll go spare!' I trembled to Petesy when the patrol car had disappeared.

'Mine too,' gulped my ex-passenger.

But it wasn't too bad. The worst bit for both of us was having to go to court and answer the charge like a couple of hardened criminals.

'Guilty,' we chorused. And then, sentence pronounced, I turned to my Dad with trembling lip. Though a big man he was a good and kindly father and never once did he raise his hand to me. He didn't need to: the rebuke of his eye and the formidable weight of his voice were enough to keep me in line. Right now his eye said it all.

When it was all over he came across to me, his jaw jutting angrily.

'Five shillings fine and a half-crown court costs, eh? You were lucky, my lad.' And then, inclining towards me ever so slightly, he fixed me with his eye and said: 'Right – you were caught, you pay the fine.'

He was a wise Dad, too.

It seemed the floodgate had been opened now and the memories were flowing freely. And as I drove back out through the town I couldn't help but stop for a moment at the top of my old street, Craigwell Avenue, for a glance back down the years.

This place was home to me for the first nineteen years of my life, and it is a hard man indeed who can return to his roots without some sort of stirring within his breast. Depending on the hallmark of those early years – whether stamped with love, hate or indifference – his memories will cause him either to rejoice or recoil at the sight of those familiar forms. A home, after all, is more than bricks and mortar. Life is indelible, and what goes on within the walls of our homes will leave its mark. Those walls, like our young minds, will absorb the colours that fill our lives, so that long after we have grown and moved on the picture that was painted by the brush-strokes of our early years will remain.

Happily, as I let my eyes rest on the little terraced house that once sheltered the Forde family, I was aware that the colours of my own childhood were mostly bright, dulled here and there only by the shadow of my mother's illness which kept her housebound for so many of the years that I was privileged to share with her and Dad and my sister Leah.

They were good years, and like every childhood mine seemed to last for ever. Never for a moment did we think we would grow out of our endless games into that other, serious world inhabited by adults. But then, suddenly, one day we had turned round and realised that the games were over. Childhood had vanished. One minute it had been there – bright and bouncy as always – the next it had flown away.

But the memories were for keeping.

As I pulled away from the kerb, taking one last peep down Memory Lane, I couldn't help thinking of another leaving: that distant February morning when, at the age of nineteen, I had said my goodbyes and stepped out of the house into a new world, a new life, a new career. I was off to join the RUC. I remember that morning so well . . .

At the end of the street I had stopped and turned to look back, and I can recall the winter sun polishing the windows and shining the grey-slate roofs as the little houses huddled together, leaning on one another against the spiteful wind. In that gentle light Craigwell Avenue had looked its best, but even that was nothing to celebrate. Then the wind had come rushing up and lashed me with its icy whip as though driving me on. I turned up my collar, glanced again at home and Mum's face behind the frosty glass, and went for the bus.

In my hands I'd had a case and a carrier bag, and packed away inside was everything I thought I would need in the days that lay ahead. And yet, as I thought back on it now, I knew that the things I had *most* needed as I'd headed out into the world on that crisp morning were the things I needed no suitcase for.

One of the last things Mum had said to me before I left the house was: 'Have you got everything you need, son?' And she must have known that if I hadn't it was too late now, anyway. For nineteen years she and Dad had cared for me, taught me, guided me, corrected me, equipped me. For nineteen years they had been entrusted with my young life and I had been theirs to mould as they wished.

I like to think they did a good job, so that when the day came for me to step out on my own the most precious thing I took with me was what they had given me: myself. For I was what a loving mother and father had made me. As my memories, so was I. And as I motored away out of Portadown that morning I recalled something I had read in my Bible study notes: 'Memory is the key to the building and development of character.'

It was a phrase that was to be underlined for me that day, for the court case at which I was to give evidence that afternoon centred around a young lad . . . and the influences in his life.

His name was Thomas and he came from one of Belfast's many Roman Catholic estates. He was seventeen years of age, which meant that ever since he could remember there had been a sort of war going on in the world outside his front door, so that to him the news of a bombing or murder was as unremarkable as the weather forecast.

In spite of this Thomas had been reared by a mother and father who wanted nothing to do with the violence; like my own parents, they had sought to teach their children decent standards of love and respect. But, as every parent knows, it is impossible to shield youngsters from outside influences, and through mixing with the wrong sort and listening to the propaganda Thomas found himself in the Fianna, the junior wing of the Provisional IRA.

I turned on to the motorway, recalling how, a few months earlier, a colleague and I had interviewed Thomas at Castlereagh Police Office. He'd been brought in for questioning on suspicion of involvement in terrorism, but clearly he was finished with that. Indeed, he wanted to make a clean breast of it, and with his co-operation we quickly established his membership of an illegal organisation. He also willingly told us how he had drilled with the Fianna, how he had collected money on behalf of the IRA for berets and other items of clothing, and how he had attended arms training sessions.

The story was a familiar one: though a decent lad at heart Thomas had been pressured from various quarters and somehow found himself being sucked down into the whirlpool of terrorism until it was easier to accede than resist.

However, Thomas's home life had stood him in good stead, because after a few months he began to realise that he ought to be having nothing to do with these people and their violence, and through the encouragement of a local priest he was introduced to the Northern Ireland Peace People. At that time this group was arranging holidays abroad for young people from both Catholic and Protestant homes, the idea being to get the youngsters out of their turbulent environment and to encourage bridge-building between the two groups. Thomas was invited to go on one of these holidays, but word got back to the Fianna and he was advised not to go.

Once again his upbringing served him well: he decided to go ahead with the holiday.

When he returned his former associates in the Fianna told him that he was to be punished with a 'wall job' (dismissal by beating), but in the event he was given a basic dismissal from his company and told not to return. This, he told us, severed his connection with the IRA, and from that day on he'd had nothing more to do with them.

But Thomas still had to face criminal charges in connection with his involvement in terrorism, and after being officially charged before a special court he was released to await trial at Crumlin Road Courthouse. As I headed down into Belfast that afternoon I wondered what the outcome would be.

Despite my little diversion down in Portadown I was in good time for the case, and as I slipped into Number Three Court I noted without surprise that Thomas's parents were already seated in the public gallery, along with the parish priest who had been so helpful in encouraging the lad to break with the terrorists. Today, I knew, would be a critical day for this young man, and it was good to see that the support he would be needing was already on hand.

And then, as I began making my way to my seat, I was called aside by Thomas's barrister. He knew that I would be called upon to give evidence and confided in me that his client would be pleading 'guilty'. In the circumstances, he went on, would I be willing to say a favourable word on the lad's behalf?

I looked him in the eye for a moment, and then said: 'You know, you're putting me in a very difficult position. I appreciate that Thomas has severed his connection with the Provos and that he intends going straight from now on, but he's here on a serious charge: you and I know that we're talking about an organisation that has murdered many people and caused much terrorism in our land.' I paused and glanced away as a door on the other side of the court swung open and the judge entered. 'Look,' I said, turning back to the barrister, 'let me think about it . . .'

Only once before had I felt free to speak on behalf of a person who had been a member of a terrorist organisation; it was not the sort of thing a policeman did lightly. But sitting there looking across the court at Thomas, and at his father beyond, I was suddenly reminded of another youngster in another age in another courthouse. The charge on that occasion had not been so serious, but that lad too had realised the error of his ways . . . and with encouragement and support he had not gone wrong again.

So, thanks to a memory, my evidence that day included a word on the accused's behalf. I don't know whether it helped, but I was hopeful that on weighing up the facts the judge would not be too hard on the young offender. I was not to be disappointed.

'Would the accused please stand.'

Thomas rose to his feet and the judge fixed him with his eye as he began: 'You started life with one of the greatest blessings any of us can have, and those of us who have it can never be sufficiently grateful for it. That is: being born into a good home, a happy home, and being given a good rearing, a good upbringing in that home. You have had good parents, good brothers and sisters, and you belong to a happy home. That will stand to you all the days of your life, even if you live to be a very old man. I hope that in time, perhaps not too soon, but in time you will get married and find a similarly happy and good home of your own, with memories of the home in which you were brought up.'

He paused and glanced at his notes before going on:

'It is noteworthy that no member of your family had ever been in trouble with the law before today. That is a negative way of putting it, but, quite apart from that, your parents have done good work in trying to do what *all* parents should do, and what all too few parents do: trying on occasions of trouble, on occasions of disorder and of possible rioting, shooting and burning and so on, to keep their children out of trouble by taking positive steps.

'I hope you will always remember that you were very young when you let yourself get involved with these people. You should be grateful to your parish priest for the way he rescued you and got you into good company, into the company of people who are trying to keep the peace and re-establish peace, and establish conditions in which all of us can get on with people of different religions from ourselves. That is desperately important.

'I am sorry to see that you say you have lost contact with the people who sent you abroad on the holiday. I hope you will re-establish contact with them, but I am not making that a condition in adjourning this case. What I am going to do is to adjourn it for a full year, and I give you my word – this will apply whether I am alive or dead, one year hence – that if you keep out of trouble in that year you will not go to jail or any other place where you will be locked up, so to speak, for a single day. I think you were in custody for about six days last summer. Well, if you go straight for the next twelve months you will not serve a single day and I will see that that is put on the record so that if another judge has to deal with it he will know that I have said I will not be hard on you. I will make it clear that you would get out in one year's time. Do you understand that?'

Thomas nodded vigorously. 'Yes, Sir.'

'Now, in case I am not here one year hence,' the judge continued, 'let me say this: just do not go straight for the next twelve months. For heaven's sake, for your family's sake, for your own sake, do that and go straight for the rest of your life in the way your father and mother have done. Now off you go.'

Then the judge turned to the clerk of the court. 'I would ask that a record be made of my recommendation and that it be recorded in the papers.'

Thomas glanced at his parents, beaming with relief and gratitude, and in that instant I knew that I'd made the right decision. Only time would tell, of course, but I quite expected Thomas's first appearance in court to be his last, too.

I had to hurry away then, for I had another important appointment, this time at home, but as I passed Thomas and his parents in the corridor outside I was gratified to see this young lad reach out his hand to grab mine. There was no need for words: his grip and his grin said it all.

Then it was down the courthouse steps and along to the car, and as I went I was aware of a victory. Not the victory of Thomas's sentence, though without doubt that was to be celebrated, but rather the victory of the memories. What was that phrase again?

'Memory is the key to the building and development of character.'

That was the real victory seen in court that day. And, strangely enough, it wasn't Thomas's triumph at all. It was his Mum and Dad's.

I pulled the car into the drive, just avoiding the mountain of bicycles stacked to one side, and emerged to the sound of pop music pummelling my windows and roars of laughter exploding from the lounge. Yes, the party was in full swing. Trifles and cakes were being ferried from one room to another by a frazzled figure under a funny hat and I called out: 'How's it going, Lily? Got a houseful?'

She rolled her eyes heavenward in a desperate gesture, glanced away, and then stopped suddenly. Taking a pace backward she turned and stared at me.

'Ben! What ever happened to your hair?'

I knew that was coming, and I was ready for it.

'Barber's special,' I said breezily. 'Two haircuts for the price of one.'

Her mouth fell open in horror and I countered: 'Just think of the money we're saving!'

The horror began to dissolve in laughter, but suddenly Lily was locked in combat with an escaping trifle. With that under control she was seized again by that desperate look and staggered on into the living room.

I took a deep breath . . . and plunged in behind her.

Keri was fourteen today and she was celebrating in style. On the drawing board it had been planned as one of those quiet little teas 'with just a few close friends', but who wants a quiet little tea when you can cram the house with half the neighbourhood and make so much noise that the jellies never get a chance to stop shaking! Parties are supposed to be fun, aren't they?

I poked my head into the lounge to get a first-hand view of my furniture and carpet being massacred, and then retreated into the kitchen where that person with the funny hat was wrestling with the orange squash bottles.

'Do you need me in here, Lily, or –' and the rest of my words were lost in a sudden whirlwind of young people clamouring for drinks. Undaunted, Lily poured the squash and stood there imitating one of her own jellies as the tide of youngsters swept past me again on its way back to the battlefield.

'What you need,' I said, taking control of the situation, 'is a nice cup of tea.'

The funny hat wobbled, and a smile appeared beneath it.

Later that night, when the celebrations were just a pile of crumbs on the carpet and we had two kids tucked up in bed, Lily and I took our cocoa and flopped on to the settee. We sat there surveying what used to be our lounge, and Lily said: 'This lot can wait till the morning.' Then: 'Did you see the cards?' And despite the late hour there was a twinkle in her eye.

I glanced across the room . . . and immediately caught on. Among Keri's birthday cards were three oversized ones – the type that come in boxes: very feminine and distinctly romantic. Then I turned to Lily, smiling.

'Our little girl's growing up,' I said.

Lily grinned, moving closer to me and slipping her arm through mine, and we sat there, savouring one of those precious moments of togetherness that come to all happy couples now and then . . . spontaneous moments that settle like gentle doves and ask nothing of us, other than that we enjoy them. For they do not last long . . . and, like doves, they are easily frightened away. So it was that we sat there saying nothing in a silence that spoke volumes. For though our lips were still, our hearts, I knew, were speaking. Together they were remembering that day exactly fourteen years ago when our Keri had arrived to brighten our lives. What joy she had brought into our home!

But along with the rejoicing had come the responsibility of raising a family in a twisted world, and so there was a sobering edge to our happiness that night: the colourful cards before our eyes reminded us that one day our children would be fully grown and leaving home. Then it would be *our* turn to ask: 'Have you got everything you need?' If they hadn't it would be our fault, not theirs.

And suddenly the doves were gone. Without thinking, I opened my mouth and startled them, and the spell was broken.

'I wonder who planted that bomb under Jim Wright's car?'

Lily turned to me, curious.

'What ever made you think of that?'

'Oh . . . something I read,' I replied.

8: '. . . as we forgive them'

It was a day for great rejoicing. For the past weekend Lily had been away at Capernwray Hall in the Lake District for a women's fellowship and teaching weekend, and today she was coming home. We had all missed her, and along with our gratitude that she was returning there was a certain amount of relief. For the kids it meant a return to 'proper food' (they'd thought their mother's cooking uninteresting until they'd tasted mine!), and for me it meant that I could exchange the housework for the more familiar and seemingly less demanding business of chasing terrorists!

'Don't get me wrong,' I said to Lily as we prised her away from her travel party and bundled her kidnap-style into the car at York Road station. 'It isn't that we didn't manage without you, love. It's just that –'

'The kids are fed up with burnt chips?'

A roar of agreement went up from our offspring as I slipped the car into gear, and Lily and I exchanged a smile of perfect understanding.

I set an easy pace on the way home, for Lily was excited about the weekend and there was much she wanted to share: little snippits from the teach-in sessions, lingering memories from the fellowship hours, and conversations with friends old and new.

It was as we were driving up past the City Hall that I first heard the name of one of these new friends, but of course at that point I had no idea that Florence Cobb was destined for the pages of this book. Come to that, who could have known just how God was going to use her a few months hence?

It was the accordion that brought us together. Florence had been sharing with Lily how she hoped to start some children's meetings in her Hillsborough home just a few miles outside Belfast, and that she was looking for a small piano accordion with which to accompany the children's singing. Lily told her that we had one we didn't use and that she was welcome to it. Providing Ben agreed.

I did. I'd bought that little instrument many years ago, not long after we'd got married. One of my colleagues was wanting to raise some money to buy his daughter a bicycle and he had an accordion he wanted to sell. I bought it for the very reasonable sum of six pounds, enthusing to Lily that if I could master the little keyboard I could use it to accompany myself at the various singing engagements that came my way.

But good intentions never taught anyone to play a musical instrument and that accordion had spent the last ten years in our loft, silent and dusty. If Florence could make good use of it she was indeed welcome to it.

'That's great, Ben,' Lily beamed. And then, a little sheepishly: 'She's coming by tomorrow to pick it up.'

'Women!' I sighed, glancing at Lily in mock reproach. 'I'll tell you what: I'll hunt out the accordion while you fix us one of your special dinners. What d'you say?'

There was a chorus of 'Please, Mum!' from the back seat, a smile from Lily, and it was settled.

As arranged, Florence collected the accordion the following morning, but I was away on a case so I didn't have the chance to meet her. That pleasure had to wait until later in the summer when both our families attended the CPA holiday week up in Portrush. Except that Florence's family was incomplete: Inspector Harold

Cobb, Florence's husband and the father of their three children, had been killed two years earlier by the IRA.

Evidently Harold was much loved by his family, for when we met them we quickly became aware of their sense of loss. But we were equally conscious of God's grace at work in their lives, as was evidenced one evening when many police families gathered for a fellowship hour in an hotel lounge and 18-year-old Alan, the Cobbs' eldest son, shared how God had given him the strength to cope with his father's death. What was even more moving, however, was Alan's attitude towards the man who took his father from him: he felt no hatred or bitterness. Although angry at first, and still deeply hurt, God, he said, had given him peace.

We got to know the Cobbs fairly well over that August holiday. I discovered that Alan and his brother Ivan (two years younger but considerably taller at 6ft 4ins!) were keen footballers like myself and were often first on the scene when a beach match had been arranged. And to my delight I found that I also had something in common with the youngest member of the family, nine-year-old Pauline: we both loved ice-cream! And there was plenty of it during that sun-filled week.

In addition, Lily and I had some lovely conversations with Florence. But even then I did not know that Florence's story would find its way into this book. That seed was planted some months later, just before Christmas, when I arrived home from work one evening to see her looking out from the television set. She was being interviewed at her home by a news reporter, and the words that came from her lips, coupled with the light in her eyes, thrilled my weary heart. For wherever I turned there seemed to be bad news – murder, hatred, vengeance – and here was a woman who had suffered the ultimate hurt at the hand of the terrorist talking about forgiveness.

It's easy to *talk* of forgiveness, of course; the word

trips easily off the tongue, and over the years the people of Northern Ireland had continually been exhorted by parson and priest to forgive their enemies. But not until now had I heard anyone doing this in public in such a positive way. Not that Florence had wanted her forgiveness of Harold's assassin to be anything other than private. As she told me later, 'It just slipped out.'

I was glad of that. It encouraged me no end to hear a widow telling the world that she had written to the man who killed her husband to say, 'I forgive you.' And telling the world she was, for the love of God (what else could it have been?) flowing through Florence made headlines in several national newspapers, and reached out across the seas via the media to America, Canada and even Australia.

At last there was some good news coming out of Ulster. At last the world was seeing that as well as hate there is love in 'Bomb City'. And it was then I knew that the Cobb family would be part of this book.

But police duty called and it wasn't until the following spring that I drove up to Hillsborough, cassette recorder on the seat beside me, to listen to the full story.

Florence's house – a handsome whitewashed bungalow set amid fields and paddocks – rests on a hill overlooking the valley of Belfast with the towering Divis Mountain beyond. Directly in front of the house, about four miles distant, the white-painted concrete blocks of the Maze Prison sprawl across the landscape, an ugly blemish on a picture postcard view. Worse still, I thought as the car crunched up the gravel road leading to the Cobb home, is the fact that the man who shot Harold (we'll call him Liam) is down there in one of those cells serving a life sentence. And I wondered how Florence felt about the constant reminder.

I pulled into the drive and Florence appeared at the door, tall and erect with her dark hair framing a welcoming face. Pauline appeared behind her, followed by Ivan. Only Alan was absent, away at work.

'But he'll be home later, Ben. He won't mind if we start on our tea.'

Hospitality, I soon learned, was a feature of the Cobb household, and while we tucked into salad and home-made cakes we chatted light-heartedly . . . and I was glad because I knew instinctively that when we got round to talking about Harold there would be no pain.

'He was a wonderful husband,' said Florence, as we settled into armchairs beside the picture windows after tea. And then, with a fond glance at Pauline clearing the table, 'And a loving father. He was a hard-working man, too. He built our home here almost single-handed, and he loved to be doing things in the garden or tinkering with the car. He never sat still. If he wasn't busy with something at home he'd be away out taking some meeting or other with the CPA – the Christian Police Association.'

She paused, glancing down at her wedding ring, and for a moment she sat fingering it, remembering . . .

Harold and Florence Cobb, I learned, became Christians in 1964. They had been married just a few years and were enjoying raising their young family and building a home. It was the traditional picture of domestic bliss. And yet they knew that something vital was missing from their lives. Apparently God used the coalman to show them what that was!

'His name was Sammy,' said Florence, smiling at the memory. 'He called at the house every Thursday, and he always carried a New Testament with him. Wherever he went he would speak about the gospel to his customers, and he talked about God's love to me on a number of occasions. But one day it was somehow different. He came in and read out of his little book from Romans 10: "Whosoever shall call upon the name of the Lord shall be saved."

99

' "You know, Florence," he said, "that 'whosoever' means you!" – and he went on to explain as before how I needed to get right with God.

'Well, I knew this; I'd known it for a long time because when I was 15 I was challenged to accept Christ as my Saviour at a crusade meeting in Belfast. But I turned away from the call, thinking that if I became a Christian I'd have to give up the cinema and dancing and all the things I enjoyed.' She laughed softly. 'You see, I didn't know about God's wonderful love at that time; I had no idea that when Jesus comes in and fills your life he brings so much joy and contentment that dancing and so on no longer satisfies.'

I nodded, smiling, and she went on: 'Well, God was very patient with me and he'd allowed me to go my own way for so long, but now as I stood there listening to Sammy I knew that God was challenging me once more, and when Harold came out to talk to Sammy I went through to the garage at the back of the house – it didn't matter where; I just had to get alone – and there I knelt down on an old piece of carpet and gave my life over to God. It was nothing dramatic, but I knew it was for real. I had a wonderful sense of God's love, and a reassuring peace.'

Five days later, Florence told me, Harold went with Sammy to a Bible Class meeting at the late Willie Mullan's church in Lurgan, and there he too committed his life to God.

'It was lovely. Suddenly we had a new dimension to our lives – a whole new purpose. We were discovering God's love, and it was exciting.'

'Oh, it gets better as you go on, Florence,' I enthused, 'as I'm sure you know. His love never pales. What does that old hymn say? "New every morning is his love." '

'And that's just what we were finding, Ben. It was too good to be true – and yet it *was* true. He truly is a loving heavenly Father.'

Eager to meet other Christians and to worship with them, Florence and Harold joined Pastor Mullan's church.

'We were both keen to serve the Lord,' Florence went on, 'and I became a teacher in the Sunday School. But it was difficult for Harold to take on any church work because of the irregular hours he was working as a police constable. But he was a keen Christian, always looking for opportunities to witness for the Lord, and he found his niche in the CPA. There were always meetings to attend and Harold would love to give his testimony. Then, of course, he would speak about his faith to the people he met in the course of his work.'

She turned to me, her eyes bright.

'You know, he had a great love for people. All people, not just those of his own background. In fact he always found it hard to understand the differences which divide Protestants and Catholics because he was from the South and never had any trouble with his Catholic neighbours there.

'Yes, he loved all men and longed for them to come to a knowledge of God. Many times I heard him pray at CPA meetings for Roman Catholic people – particularly for members of the IRA.

'He never hated anybody, whatever label they wore. He believed that we ought to love our enemies, as the Bible would have all men do, and in that sense he was a far stronger Christian than I. He had tremendous faith in his God and really it was his influence that set me on my feet as far as the Christian life was concerned. His was such a practical, down-to-earth faith: something, I suppose, which developed in relation to the type of work he was doing.'

I nodded. 'That's for sure,' I said. 'You see life in the raw in this job, and it's not a pretty sight. Harold would have known that you need a strong, basic faith in those circumstances. And for all of us that includes times of danger.'

I wasn't surprised to hear that Harold knew all about danger. In 1973 he was promoted to sergeant and the increased responsibilities also meant increased risks because by this time the present IRA campaign was well underway and Harold's posting was with the Special Patrol Group (the RUC's uniformed front-line action group) in the 'bandit country' of Armagh.

'He had a number of near misses while he was with the SPG,' said Florence, 'but I didn't know about them until afterwards, which is just as well because I'm a worrier. On quite a few occasions I cried myself to sleep, wondering whether he would be coming home the next morning. But, you know, God is good and he always brought Harold home safe and sound – until that last day, of course.'

She glanced away, hesitating for but a moment. And then she said: 'But I believe Harold's appointed time had come. God allowed it because his work was finished and he was being called home.'

I met her eyes, nodding, unsure of what to say. Florence Cobb, it seemed to me, was a remarkable lady. But no, I knew she would not approve of that thought. She would say that if anyone was remarkable it was her God, for he was the source of her composure and her peace. And as if to underline that fact, and to ease my diffidence, she said: 'If it would help, I'll show you where it happened.'

And so we set out beneath a late sun, Florence, Pauline and myself (Ivan had a previous engagement), motoring through the long shadows of the country lanes, sweeping down between the whispering fields and watching trees, and on into Lurgan. On the face of it, it was a curious excursion: our destination the place where a man died. But there was nothing morbid or callous about our motives, and as we bowled into the town any misgivings I'd had when we started out had evaporated. The only apprehension was perhaps that of entering a town that has long been a trouble-spot in the ongoing battle with the terrorists. But it is all too easy to give the wrong impression of a place, and as we drove slowly through the High Street Florence was quick to point out that the great majority of Lurgan's inhabitants are good, decent people. As in so many parts of the world today, however, there is a minority here who have no desire for peace, and it is those people who have given the town a bad name. Those trouble-makers have also made it necessary for the High Street to be sealed off at night by barriers. Before those barriers were erected there were frequent car-bomb attacks on shops and other premises, and among the many buildings destroyed in this way was the police station. Florence pointed it out as we passed by – a sorry heap of rubble between two shops – and then indicated the town hall.

'That's where the police operate from now,' she said. 'They didn't think it worth rebuilding the station just to have it blown up again.'

Another evidence of the hostilities which continue to plague Lurgan from time to time is the need for the presence of soldiers. There is an army station nearby, and when we eased to a halt near the lower end of the High Street it was under the wary eyes of a five-man foot patrol. The shops having just closed, the soldiers were moving down through the town-centre on what appeared to be a routine scouting mission.

We stepped from the car as the troops passed the Church Place barrier and moved on into one of the Catholic quarters.

Florence nodded in that direction and said: 'That's where it happened.'

There is an island in the middle of the road at Church Place, and with Florence leading the way we crossed over and stood there in the dying light of the sunset, our eyes fixed on the spot where Harold fell. He had been stationed in Lurgan for just a few months, posted here after his promotion to Inspector the previous summer. Without flinching, Florence told me how it happened.

'Some of the traders had been complaining that the barriers weren't being opened on time in the morning, so on this particular day Harold went first to the Queen Street barrier and then down here to Church Place to make sure the street was open at the proper time, eight thirty. He was standing talking to the constables on duty when gunmen opened fire from what was then a derelict café – over there.'

She pointed to the place, now rebuilt as a drinking club, about fifty yards from the barrier.

'They used to shoot at the policemen from down in the Catholic quarters – one man was killed shortly before Harold was posted here – but then the police put up sheets of corrugated iron sixteen feet high, so if the terrorists wanted to shoot at them they had to come into the High Street. And that's what happened. The gunmen came round the back of the High Street and through the derelict building and opened fire from the doorway.'

Apparently high-powered rifles were used – the type that can kill at two miles – so Harold, who had his back to them at the time, stood no chance. He was killed instantly by one bullet in the back of the head. His two colleagues were also hit and wounded.

'It's strange,' said Florence, turning to me, 'but I think he knew he was going to die. And perhaps, in a way, I too had been warned.'

I stared at her. 'Oh?'

'Yes. The previous morning, when Harold left the house, I was lying in bed when suddenly I was gripped with panic and felt I had to run out and warn him to look under the car in case there was a bomb. But when I got to the front door I saw the car pulling away and I knew it was a false alarm. That had never happened to me before. Of course, we'd always tried to be security conscious, as anyone in our situation would, but I'd never known such an impulse before.'

'And what about Harold?' I said. 'What makes you think he knew?'

'Well, I don't know for sure. But that evening Harold was taking a CPA meeting and at the last minute he changed the hymns he had selected earlier, choosing instead "Face to Face with Christ My Saviour" and "When We All Get to Heaven". I think he had a premonition.'

We did not linger in Lurgan. We had seen what we had come to see, and to my mind there was nothing to be gained by asking Florence to tell me more while standing there only yards from where Harold died. Regardless of her willingness to show me the place, and the evident peace which ruled in her heart, I suspected that it had cost her something to revive the memories. And in that case there was no need to make her pay more dearly than was necessary.

'Come on,' I said, 'I know a decent little café where we can have a coffee.' And then, glancing at Pauline: 'Tasty fish suppers, too!'

'Ben!' cried Florence in gentle reproach. 'She'll go off bang.'

I glanced at her, smiling. We're all kids at heart. 'Now don't tell me,' I said, 'that you couldn't look at a bag of chips!'

And we all laughed, and it was good, so we hopped into the car and headed out of the faint cloud that had drifted over our minds, into the last orange flare of the disappearing sun.

The place I had in mind was a little fish-bar in Portadown. I had been looking for an excuse to call in there ever since I'd noticed it on my way out of the town that morning I'd visited Jim Wright's widow. The proprietors, the McCann brothers, had shared my childhood years, and in those days their father managed the place. I had always been indebted to Mr McCann because he once saved me from injury in what could have been a nasty accident.

My sister Leah and I had been sent to fetch some milk from the dairy which stood near a local bridge. We arrived there a few minutes before the place was due to open, and while we were waiting a tractor and hay-float came trundling by on the other side of the road. With nothing better to do I ran across and leapt on to the back of the float, intending to take a short ride over the bridge and then to jump off and run back to Leah. But I didn't hear the lorry approaching from the opposite direction, and when I shot out from behind the float it was straight into the path of the truck.

The effect was not unlike that of a tennis ball meeting a racquet! I bounced off the lorry into the side of the road . . . where I fell straight into the arms of Mr McCann. He just happened to be passing by!

Thinking back on it, I reckoned the least I could do by way of gratitude was to patronise the McCanns' little eating-house now and then. This evening seemed a good opportunity. It was a fair distance from Lurgan, of course, but there was still enough light in the sky to allow us the benefit of the local scenery. And as we sped through the streets and up on to the Portadown road Florence told me about that morning when she received the news of Harold's death.

'It was about ten o'clock in the morning. I was setting the fire when I heard the doorbell, and as soon as I opened the door and saw three members of Lurgan RUC standing there I knew what had happened.

'But it was wonderful, Ben, because straightaway the Lord was there beside me, breathing peace into my heart. He completely removed all panic and gave me instead this incredible calm. It was beautiful.'

But Florence was quick to point out that the peace she

was given to help her cope with her crisis did not remove the hurt. How could it?

'I shed many, many tears in private, and I went through all the dark tunnels of emotion – loneliness, depression, self-pity – but you destroy yourself if you allow those feelings to get a hold of you. I needed help and, as so often happens, I found it in God's promise – that wee verse in the Psalms: "I will be a father unto the fatherless and a comfort unto the widow." '

'What about the kids?' I said. 'How did they cope?'

'They went through their own grief, of course. Alan was 15 at the time, Ivan 13 and Pauline six, and they all loved their Daddy very much. But the Lord sustained us all and brought us out of it without bitterness.'

I smiled across at her. 'You found God to be as good as his word.'

'I did, Ben. We all did.' And she paused before she went on: 'You know, until it happens to you, you just can't imagine how real his presence can be, and just how practical his help is. I can honestly say that he *was* a father to the fatherless. He helped me bring up the children. When I needed him he was there.'

We rolled into Portadown in the last of the daylight and a minute or two later Florence and Pauline were settling in behind one of the fish-bar tables while I ordered three helpings of fish and chips. (Florence couldn't resist them once she caught a whiff of the deep-fryer!) It was Jack McCann who was behind the counter that evening, and while the batter was crisping up he and I exchanged a few words about old times. Then it was across to the table and three hungry travellers were tucking into their supper, mouthfuls punctuated by various noises of appreciation.

We washed the whole lot down with hot, sweet tea, and then I turned to Florence with another question.

'You were telling me about how the children coped

107

with Harold's death,' I said. 'Did they have a faith of their own?'

Florence nodded. 'The boys were already committed Christians when their father died –'

'And I gave my heart to the Lord the following summer,' Pauline cut in. 'At a tent crusade, when Dick Saunders came to Lisburn.'

'Always a lady's prerogative to be last,' I smiled. 'Tell me, do you keep your mum company when your big brothers are out, Pauline?'

She grinned, nodded, and Florence glanced affectionately across at her little girl. 'She does, Ben. And, you know, that's another of God's blessings. Harold and I could never understand why the Lord kept us waiting so long for Pauline, but now I see that it was his goodness. As you say, Alan and Ivan are out a great deal now – Alan at work and Ivan at college, and they're often out in the evening – but Pauline is always around. She's my little companion.' Another smile in Pauline's direction. 'If she'd arrived when Harold and I had wanted her, she too would be grown up by now and I'd be on my own a lot more.

'That's something else we had to learn: that God's timing is always right.'

It was all but fully dark when we motored back into Hillsborough that night, and as we got out of the car in the driveway I found my eyes being drawn beyond the dim garden and the veiled fields to the valley below where a mass of brilliant orange lights twinkled at me in a deceptive splash of brightness.

For a moment I stood there in silence, and then Florence was by my side.

'Someone said it looked like Fairyland,' she said. 'But nothing could be further from the truth, could it.'

As a policeman working in Belfast I am all too familiar with those lights: they are the perimeter arc-lamps surrounding the Maze Prison. And I wondered again whether the constant reminder of the man who shot the beloved husband and father worried them. A moment later that thought found its way past my lips and out into the night air. It was a question I hadn't meant to ask.

'No, the lights don't worry us,' said Florence in the darkness. 'There are plenty of things to remind us of Harold around the home, so seeing those lights every time I draw the curtains doesn't make any difference. We're very aware that God is with us every hour of every day, and that has been so tremendously uplifting that feelings are overshadowed. Besides, as I've said, I've no bitterness towards Liam.'

Behind us the front door was opened by Alan, now home from work, and in the wedge of yellow light that fell around us from the hallway we exchanged greetings and then stepped into the house.

'Let's get the kettle on,' said Florence, heading for the kitchen. 'Coffee for everyone? What about you, Pauline? Are you away to bed?'

By the size of the yawn that came over Pauline I guessed she wouldn't need any prompting, and after goodnight kisses (even one for 'Uncle Ben'!) she was away to her room.

'Hey, Ben, are you into cameras?' said Alan.

'Who, me?' I said, glancing round as though he might have been asking someone else. Ben is definitely not into cameras.

'I'm all right with a nice, simple one where all you have to do is press the button,' I confessed. 'But I'm not much good with those multi-gadgeted things.'

He looked a little disappointed so I was quick to add: 'But I'm always willing to learn.'

He smiled the smile of the reprieved and went off to fetch his latest photographic acquisition, which arrived at the same time as the coffee. It was a camera. Well, that was the general idea.

'Standard 50 mill. lens, of course. Automatic override on focus. Electronic-eye exposure – computerised. Plus all the usual facilities: depth-of-field guide, multi-coated lens, delayed action, double-exposure . . . and, of course, you can get the usual range of interchangeable lenses, bayonet fitting.'

I smiled politely. 'Very impressive,' I said, just a shade tongue-in-cheek. 'But has it got a button for taking pictures?'

He glanced at me uncertainly . . . and then collapsed in laughter.

'That's right, Ben,' said Florence, handing round the coffee. 'Keep it simple. I'm glad I'm not the only one who doesn't understand all those buttons and knobs and things.'

'It *is* simple,' protested Alan, still laughing. And then, with a frown: 'But there is one thing I don't understand about this automatic exposure . . .' And he went off in search of the handbook, mumbling about apertures and other mysteries.

In the gentle light of the lamp-stand Florence and I sat on in silence, sipping from chunky stoneware coffee mugs, and I found myself admiring that lovely room: Harold Cobb's handiwork. It was a comfortable lounge, L-shaped and spacious with a rugged stone fireplace as the centre-piece: the sort of room any wife would have been proud of. And I guessed that it had been in this room, probably at the dark-oak dining table, that Florence had written that letter forgiving the man who took Harold from her. She did not do it without first consulting her children, for they had lost their father and had a right to disapprove of the letter, but apparently they had all been in agreement with it. It was written about two and a half years after Harold's death.

'But it wasn't a sudden thing,' Florence explained.

'I'd known for about six months that I had to write it.' She glanced at me. 'Ben, I know some people don't understand what I did, but God put this burden in my heart that I had to tell Liam about the Saviour's love for him, just as Sammy, the coalman, had a burden to tell us.'

I nodded, and she went on:

'Well, over the months I started that letter many, many times, but I couldn't seem to put down on paper what I wanted to say. Then the hunger strike started – the first hunger strike by IRA prisoners – and Liam was one of the seven men chosen to fast. When I realised this I felt even more compelled to write. I saw his picture on the television news one night and I just knew that the time was right. Alan and Ivan were out and Pauline was away to bed, and so I sat down to write the letter and this time the words came without any trouble.'

'Even so,' I ventured, 'it couldn't have been an easy letter to write. What did you tell Liam?'

She shifted in her seat, glancing away for a moment, but there was a light in her eyes as she replied: 'I simply told him of the Saviour's love for him and that God wanted to forgive him. But, of course, it was no good me telling him that if he thought I still held Harold's death against him, so I told him that I'd forgiven him. That's all there was to it.' She smiled. 'You see, it wasn't as though it was a difficult thing to do: it was what God wanted of me and he gave me the grace to do it.'

'Where God guides he provides,' I remarked.

'That's it. God met my need in that area just as he meets them in all other areas of our lives. There's nothing special about me that I could forgive Liam: it's *God's* forgiveness, *God's* love working through me. All the credit is his.'

I nodded. 'How did the media get hold of the story? Originally you wanted to keep it quiet, I know.'

'I did, Ben. But I discovered that God had other plans.

It came about after I'd had a call from the RUC Press Office saying that someone from one of the national newspapers wanted to interview an Ulster widow, particularly one who in some way was connected with the hunger strikers. They wanted to put my name forward, so I agreed, and the next day a reporter came up to the house. It was during that interview that I accidentally let slip about the letter I'd written.'

'But I seem to recall that they got it wrong,' I said.

'Unfortunately, they did. When the report appeared the next morning I was misquoted as saying that I'd written to Liam, begging him to end his fast, which wasn't true. I'd merely told him that I thought it would be a waste if he were to throw his life away like that; that he would only be committing suicide.'

It seemed that God was in control, however. As Florence explained, she had more than ample opportunity to put the record straight. The media quickly latched on to the published report and Florence had been at work only ten minutes that morning when she received the first of a string of telephone calls from many other newspapers, as well as from Radio Ulster and the television networks. All requested an interview.

'The first of those interviews went out on Radio Ulster at eleven o'clock that morning,' Florence recalled, 'and then at lunchtime I had to come home to meet the television people, and those interviews went out that evening on the News.

'A few days later I had a call from NBC, the American television people, and they came down for an interview, and later I heard that the programme had been seen in Australia and Canada as well as the States.'

'That's quite a response,' I remarked.

She smiled at my understatement.

'Well, Ben, I was amazed. I suppose at first I wondered what all the fuss was about, but then I realised that to the media people, who are so used to the deaths and the bitterness, this was something different. I don't think they quite understood, but they were too intrigued to let the story pass them by.'

'What about the reporters?' I enquired. 'How did they react?'

'I had a very mixed response. One woman couldn't have cared less – a very hard-bitten type. Another had tears in her eyes as I was relating about the love of God to her. And another, a man who told me he was an atheist and a humanist, phoned me the next day to tell me he'd had a sleepless night, thinking about what I'd said.

'By this time, of course, I realised that God was at work in the middle of all this.'

I smiled at her. 'I think that's one thing we can say without fear of contradiction, Florence.'

As we talked on I learned that many people up and down the country and throughout the length and breadth of Britain were so deeply moved by the love of God expressed in Florence's action that many wrote to her, most of them having pieced together an approximate address through information gleaned from the media. One lady, writing from Yorkshire, addressed her letter to: 'Mrs. Florence Cobb, Near the Maze, Belfast, Ireland.' Several others wrote 'c/o Lisburn RUC Station', where Florence works as a typist, while a man from Croydon, Surrey, utilised a description offered by his daily paper: 'Mrs. Florence Cobb, Whitewashed Bungalow, Atop a Small Hill, Outskirts of Hillsborough, Belfast, Northern Ireland.'

'I had many kind letters from people all over, Ben, and you're welcome to see them; they're a delight. They came from people on both sides of the divide in Ireland, Catholics and Protestants, all of them overflowing with love and concern for us as a family, and some of them containing very kind gifts of money. There was a lovely letter from a fellowship in England, too, enclosing a very

113

generous gift which was the result of their offering one Sunday. Apparently they felt they should send it to us, which was very loving. But, you know, at first I wasn't happy about accepting those gifts; after praying about it, though, I realised that God could use that cash to help bring the gospel to many other prisoners in our Ulster prisons, and that money has now gone towards buying Christian literature for prison outreach.'

Then I learned that one of those letters was particularly precious to Florence. Though every letter was appreciated, there was one for which she felt specially thankful to God.

'You know, Ben, when these things happen to you, when you're the centre of so much attention, you begin to get an exaggerated opinion of yourself, and this happened to me. I'm only human and I'm afraid I began to feel intoxicated by my own importance.' She smiled coyly. 'It was going to my head a wee bit. But then I had this lovely letter from Derick Bingham, of the Crescent Church in Belfast. I think you know him.'

I nodded. Derick and I were old friends.

'Well, this letter was telling me how his people had been praying for me at the Tuesday night Bible Class, and along with the letter he sent a copy of his book, *Sure as Sunrise* – a book of daily readings. Inside he'd got all his Bible Class to sign their names, all three hundred and fifty of them!'

I grinned. 'That sounds like the Derick I know.'

'Well, that was a lovely thought,' Florence went on, 'but the point is this: that wee book arrived on December 19, when I was at the peak of my little moment of fame, and when I opened up the book to the reading for that day . . . well, let me read it to you.'

She slipped out of the room and returned moments later, leafing through the pages of the book.

'Here it is' she said, and came and sat beside me.

'Forgive me, Lord
When
Fraternising with
Fame, and
Rubbing shoulders with
Fellows who are famous
Means more than this –
The pinnacle of privilege
Fellowship with the King of Kings
And Lord of Lords –
That heartfelt handclasp and
"Inner circle" intimacy of
Being deemed a
Friend of God.'

'I see Derick is quoting a local lass there,' I said. 'Alexandra Fay Hetherington, Lisburn, County Down.'

'And I'm grateful to her, Ben. That wee poem really humbled me. You see, I felt I was beginning to forget that it was God who had put me in that position, that it was God who was using me, and that I should be just an instrument in his hand.'

'It seems you were brought down to earth with a bump,' I ventured, and Florence grinned.

'I'm glad I was. I needed that reminder from the Lord. For a moment I'd allowed things to get out of perspective, thinking how grand it was to be the centre of attraction, instead of thanking God for the tremendous privilege of being used by him to show his love to others.' She paused. 'That's a lesson I'll not easily forget.' And then she turned to me. 'In fact, Ben, this whole experience has been unforgettable. God is so good.'

'Of that there's no doubt,' I said.

A few minutes later, outside in the brittle air of the spring night, I opened the passenger door of the car and slid the cassette recorder on to the seat. And then, just as I was about to say something, my eye was caught by those blazing lights down in the valley.

'My, they really are bright,' I said.

From the doorway of the house Florence said: 'It's because it's so dark tonight, Ben. The darker the night, the brighter they shine.'

I glanced round at her, but I could no longer see her face for she stood silhouetted against the yellow glow from the hall.

'That sounds like a good line for a song,' I said. 'The darker the night, the brighter the light.'

'Like God's love,' she said.

And though her face was lost to me, I knew there was a smile on it.

Thankfully, that first hunger strike was called off before any of the seven lost their lives. To the best of my knowledge Liam has not been on another fast and he is continuing to serve his sentence for the murder of Harold Cobb. No one seems to know just what he thought of the letter he received from Florence, but I understand that it caused quite a stir in the Maze. The prisoners have their own means of sending messages round the prison – they use spoons to tap out a code on the pipes – and apparently the pipes were pretty busy that night. Take it from me, hardened IRA men are not easily unsettled, but following the arrival of that letter questions were being asked.

'How can this woman forgive the man who murdered her husband?'

'What is this salvation she talks about?'

And at least one inmate is known to have approached a Christian within the prison, wanting to know how *he* could experience this forgiveness . . . and know something of this extraordinary thing called love in 'Bomb City'.

Postscript

Murder never takes a holiday. There is never a day when the people of Northern Ireland can rise with the dawn and say, 'Today nobody will die.' For the campaign of violence lurches on, staggering from one outrage to another, and nobody can tell when the bullet and the bomb will strike again. Here in Ulster we have learned to take nothing for granted in the day that lies ahead, and to be thankful when we can retire to our beds without hearing of another death.

No, murder never takes a holiday. But the policeman must . . .

Menorca had lived up to its glossy-brochured promise, and two weeks of sun-scorched days and cool Mediterranean nights had left us refreshed and relaxed, not to mention somewhat lighter in the pocket. But every penny, I knew, was an investment. On the outside we had film-star tans to justify the expense, but the real measure of our holiday, for me at least, was what had been gained within: a welcome respite from the pressures of living a policeman's life in 'Bomb City'. I suppose I could think of a dozen ways of elaborating on that statement, but I'll settle for this: in Menorca I didn't have to carry a gun.

But now the days had been swallowed up, like all those ice-cream cocktails, and we were heading home.

There had been clear skies all the way, and for hour

upon hour we had been able to gaze down at a sun-kissed fairyland with sparkling rivers and toy-town houses. But as to the identity of those distant lands this high-flying detective was without a clue! All was not lost, however, for sitting beside me, in the guise of Lily, was an armchair travelogue. With a truly awe-inspiring talent for juggling flying time, geographical features and directional instinct, my wife was proving to me yet again that she was more than just a pretty face and periodically stating our location with all the brash confidence of a wartime navigator on a night-time bombing run to Berlin.

'How *do* you do it, Lily?' I asked in amazement, but the only answer I received was a pearly-white grin and a chuckle from the children.

'No matter,' I returned. 'I'll know when I'm home.'

'How, Dad?' said Clive, falling headlong into my little joke.

'Why, son,' I teased, 'have you been schooled all these years and don't know that Ireland is green?'

Green she is, and radiant. For all the wounds inflicted by a terrorist campaign, my homeland still wears the most beautiful face. Scarred she may be, but to me she is of matchless countenance, a queen among the nations. Hers is a rare beauty: not garish, like the sultry temptress, but fresh-faced and innocent, like the bright-eyed village lass whose comeliness grows ever richer with the ripening years.

And she belongs to us, just as we belong to her. Oh yes, we could leave her for a season, as we had done, but she was in our blood and we could not stay away for long. Sooner or later we would need to return, and return we would. Back to the hills and the loughs and the flowing fields . . . and the ugly deeds of the men of violence.

'Dad, I know another way of telling we're home.'

By now our plane was sliding in over the crystal waters

of Lough Neagh, west of Belfast. A few minutes and we would be touching down. Beyond the tiny portholes the fields and farms rushed up to greet us, filling our eyes and gladdening our hearts.

'What way is that, son?'

'Easy. Listen for Shane barking.'

Sure enough, our flight path would be taking us directly over our home, and the thought of that floppy-eared hound stirred memories and smiles which needed no words to complete them.

But then, below us, yet another means of identifying our homeland crept into view. This one, however, did not come packaged with fond thoughts . . . only sobering reality.

'Look at it,' I said to Lily. 'One big eyesore.'

They were scrawled on the landscape like some grotesque graffiti: the white-painted H-shapes of the prison blocks within the Maze. And as we flew overhead, losing height by the second now, I wondered what the unaware visitor would make of the H-blocks. Perhaps, I mused, he would wonder what they stood for.

But we knew. How could we ever forget?

On Tuesday of the next week I returned to work with a bounce. The holiday had put a spring in my step! But the Duty Inspector soon got my feet back on the ground.

'Ben, I'd like you to get over to Tennent Street and join up with the team there.'

'What's the case, sir?'

He glanced at his clip-board. 'Murder of a man named Norman Maxwell. Body found in the north of the city last Saturday night. You can familiarise yourself with the details when you get there.'

Tennent Street RUC Station is situated between the notorious Shankill and Crumlin Roads, so it was straight back into the deep end. There was no question of being gently eased back into the job immediately after the break. Like I said, murder never takes a holiday, and the investigation of such crimes would not wait for me to get acclimatised again. The gun was back on the hip, and no messing.

I decided to drive through the city and head straight up the Shankill to where Tennent Street shelters in the shadow of the Divis Mountain. So here I was, surrounded once again by the troubles . . . and yet thankful that I had only to lift my eyes to see the Mighty Hills of God. And there, right at the top, as though growing out of the mountain, stood the local TV transmitter, pointing like a solitary finger into the heavens.

'Well, Lord,' I breathed, 'here we go again. I just thank you that you're in control.' And as I turned off by the old cinema into Tennent Street I wondered what lay in store for me today.

Minutes later I was inside the station, exchanging jokes about the sun-tan with my fellow officers, and then it was down to business. I ran my eye over the murder log to acquaint myself with the details surrounding the victim's death, and after a quick briefing it was: 'Ben, will you team up with Eddie. Call with the father of the deceased and see if he can give us any leads.'

And so off we went to knock on the door . . . only to find that it opened on to one of God's little surprises.

Mr Thomas Maxwell was a charming man, and amazing with it. For his 79 years he was remarkably light on his feet, and he had a mental agility to match. But on top of that there was something else: as we stood there talking on his doorstep I was aware of a gentle light burning in his eye . . . a light that somehow shone through even the dark tears of grief.

But we were there to do a job.

'Would you mind coming along to the station with us, Mr Maxwell? We realise how painful it must be for you at this time, but we'd appreciate your help in answering some questions about your son.'

He came quite happily, and at Tennent Street he quickly adapted to the sometimes intimidating surroundings of armed policemen, steel shutters and all the other indications of the ongoing battle with the terrorist. Indeed, he was quick to make conversation about these things, and when it came to answering our many questions about his son's life and last hours he did so tirelessly. It seemed nothing would daunt this man.

And then we found out why.

'I'm a Christian. Committed my life to God nearly 60 years ago,' he beamed through moist eyes. 'In fact I was born again on the same day I was born.'

'Sounds Irish enough,' I remarked.

'That's right,' he said. 'I was born on November 26, 1903, and born again on November 26, 1923. How about that!'

Well, it cheered my heart no end to meet a man who so delighted in God, and on my first day back to work, too. Clearly, here was the hand of God encouraging me.

But Mr Maxwell wasn't through yet. Despite the tears the light was burning bright, and he went on to talk with much pleasure of God's goodness to him down the years.

What an amazing man this was. Three days ago his son had died a most brutal death, and here he was, speaking of how good God had been to him. By comparison my own faith seemed weak, as though I were just a beginner. I shared as much with him.

'Listen,' he said, his old face creasing in a benign smile. 'Norman's death doesn't alter the fact that God loves me, or that I love him. God didn't kill my son; that was the work of the devil.' A tear escaped and hurried down his cheek, but he went on: 'What does the Scripture say? "Hath not the God of all the earth done right?" He has always done right by me and I trust him to deal rightly with Norman.'

The last few words were caught away in a little spasm

of grief and I sat in silence as he dabbed at his brimming eyes with a handkerchief. A moment or two later he glanced up at me again, his composure regained, his light still bright.

'Regarding Norman's death –' he began, and then had to clear his throat. 'Regarding Norman's death I wish to make it clear on behalf of my family that we are not seeking personal vengeance on the perpetrators of this crime.'

I nodded, and was about to speak, having been reminded of those powerful words of Jesus when on the cross: 'Father, forgive them . . .' But as I glanced across at Mr Maxwell I realised he hadn't finished.

'No, we seek no vengeance. Rather we would hope that the Spirit of God would work in the hearts of those responsible and that they would be saved for all eternity.'

That first day back in Belfast turned out to be a long one, and when finally I turned the car for home that evening the August sun was beginning to fade. Darkness was gnawing at the edge of the day and soon it would devour the last trace of light.

But driving up out of the city it occurred to me that the passing of the daylight hours never worries us because we know that in God's plan of things he does not allow the darkness to rule for long. Perhaps some nights will seem longer than others, but none is interminable. Always the sun rises again to scatter the darkness before it. Always there is a dawn.

And that, I suppose, is the message of this book. Personal sorrow and distressing circumstances bring their own kind of darkness, that's for sure. But it is my conviction, borne out by the experience of some of the people who have shared the pages of this book with me, that such darkness cannot abide when the sunshine of God's love appears on the horizon.

This is not to make light of the distress which sadly

is the lot of far too many people in my homeland. But it is an affirmation that God's word is true: 'Nothing can ever separate us from the love of God.' Just as the blackest night is unable to keep us from tomorrow's daybreak, so the troubles around us will not be able to prevent us from entering into the love that for ever flows to us from the outstretched hands of Jesus on the cross.

Of course, in a land which for so long has been divided by hatred it may seem that love is powerless. Certainly it is true that hatred is a formidable force, and it will surely destroy this land without any help from the IRA.

Love, however, is stronger than hate, and there is a power in the blood of Jesus against which no malevolence can stand.

But love, like any gift, has to be received. And that is God's only condition: that we should be willing, like Jennie, Jean, Florence and so many others, to open our heart to the heart of God.

And when we do that, things will begin to happen.

For love is more powerful than any bomb, more effective than any bullet. And when, under God's hand, it 'explodes' in Northern Ireland, it will spread faster than the flames of any incendiary device.

Look for it. It is already there. It may be staring you in the face, or you may come upon it suddenly. But one thing is for sure: you'll know it when you see it.

It's unmistakable.

It's love in 'Bomb City'.

Finally, some Scriptures I would like to share with you:

Overwhelming victory is ours through Christ who loved us enough to die for us. For I am convinced that nothing can ever separate us from his love. Death can't, and life can't. The angels won't, and all the powers of hell itself cannot keep God's love away. Our fears for today, our worries about tomorrow, or where we are – high above the sky, or in the deepest ocean – nothing will ever be able to separate us from the love of God demonstrated by our Lord Jesus Christ when he died for us.

–Romans 8:37–39

God showed how much he loved us by sending his only Son into this wicked world to bring to us eternal life through his death. In this act we see what real love is: it is not our love for God, but his love for us when he sent his Son to satisfy God's anger against our sins.

–1 John 4:9,10

What a wonderful God we have – he is the Father of our Lord Jesus Christ, the source of every mercy, and the one who so wonderfully comforts and strengthens us in our hardships and trials. And why does he do this? So that when others are troubled, needing our sympathy and encouragement, we can pass on to them the same help and comfort God has given us.

–2 Corinthians 1:3,4

BEN FORDE is a serving policeman of over twenty two years in Northern Ireland's Royal Ulster Constabulary. For the past fourteen years as a Detective Constable he has been attached to the CID dealing with some of the most horrific terrorist murders to reach the newspaper headlines. His enquiries have brought him face to face with the hardest, most dedicated people known as terrorists. He has seen and experienced much grief, and many of his colleagues have been blown to death, but he has also seen the golden thread of love and reconciliation flowing from God through men. In the midst of evil, uncertainty, and physical danger God's love is triumphant. A heart-warming but challenging story which leaves the reader in no doubt as to man's only real hope—Jesus Christ.

Ben Forde has also written *Hope in 'Bomb City'*, and lives and works in Belfast.

0 551 00956 X   £1.60 net

✿marshalls